Have You Ever?

A FAIRYTALE OF A DIFFERENT VARIETY

Alicia Knecht

TRILOGY CHRISTIAN PUBLISHERS

TUSTIN, CA

Trilogy Christian Publishers
A Wholly Owned Subsidary of Trinity Broadcasting Network
2442 Michelle Drive
Tustin, CA 92780

Have You Ever?

Rights Department, 2442 Michelle Drive, Tustin, CA 92780.

Trilogy Christian Publishing/TBN and colophon are trademarks of Trinity Broadcasting Network.

Cover design by Jeff Summers

For information about special discounts for bulk purchases, please contact Trilogy Christian Publishing.

Manufactured in the United States of America

10 9 8 7 6 5 4 3 2 1

Library of Congress Cataloging-in-Publication Data is available.

ISBN: 978-1-64773-983-6

E-ISBN: 978-1-64773-984-3

Dedication

To my family, whose fierce belief in me and support is unmatched. Thank you for always being a steady place to anchor, faithful helping hands, and choosing to see possibility and goodness even when I sometimes cannot. May I always return that same kindness and blessing toward you and others.

To my friends, who walked alongside me through many of these stories, your prayers, unwavering faith, and encouragement have been a firm example of "iron sharpens iron." I am forever grateful for your presence in my life.

To my Good Lord, forever first and my greatest love of all. Without You, these pages and my fairytale would cease to exist. There is no one like You.

Publish his glorious deeds among the nations. Tell everyone about the amazing things he does.

—Psalm 96:3 (NLT)

Contents

Prologue

Welcome to the story of my life, or at least part of it, that is! Before we dive into this untold adventure, let me clarify a few things. First, I am just an ordinary girl. (Which now you are probably wondering why you even want to read this book. Ha! But hang on, I promise it gets good.) I grew up in a small town in Indiana that most folks cannot find on the map. For most of my life, I have felt awkward, self-conscious, like I don't fit, and am not "put together." You know those people you look at, and they seem to look put together? I am not one of those, especially in the fashion department. There are those rare days, though, when I feel brilliant. Other days, I try to exit my vehicle with my seatbelt still fastened. Yes, and that has happened not once but multiple times in my life. As one of my favorite Bible teachers likes to say, "I am blonder than I pay to be." I can assure you that applies to this gal too.

Secondly, anything you read from here on out is only extraordinary because the Lord got involved. Our lives are filled with perceived ordinary moments, but when He starts moving in your life, you better believe it is anything but that!

Thirdly, to protect the individuals who have graced the landscape of my story, they will remain anonymous. My heart is never to dishonor or hurt anyone. Our lives are full of characters, some God-ordained, and others we choose from our moments of impaired judgment or brokenness. Nonetheless, they are all important and can impact the trajectory of our lives immensely.

Lastly, my prayer is that this book helps open your eyes to see God in your own story and that you will feel less alone in your life and walk of faith. I pray it also equips you for your journey, which is why every chapter ends with Bible verses to declare and a prayer. You can read this from beginning to end or pick a chapter that speaks to you whenever you need it. However, there is no substitution for your Bible so make sure you open yours, allow God to speak to you through His Word, and highlight verses as you go!

May these God stories fill you with hope and stir a new faith in you to take God at His Word and believe He is working and fashioning the events of your life into an epic tale far better than any fairytale. He is using every facet to help you become who He has always dreamed you would be. May your story be sent forth as well to be a breath of fresh air for someone else. We all love a good story, right? We are in this together—through laughter, tears, joy, celebration, loss, and love.

Shall we?

CHAPTER 1

The Beginning

I wanna see something I've not seen, something so big, I wanna be a part of something great. It takes a miracle to do. We, Your children, wanna do something big for you!

—John Waller

Many may not consider this a fairytale, but as the pages flutter from chapter to chapter, a familiar storyline will arise. Yet our God stories are incredibly more profound and whimsical. We have a guaranteed better ending and happily ever after because we belong to the King of Kings. There are many stories that I could tell but let's start with the following to bring you up to speed.

A long, long time ago (ten years to be exact, and if you sang that previous line like the oldie's song "American Pie," you get extra kudos!), I was watching my life crumble. My career wasn't heading in the right direction, and if anything, it looked like that situation might get worse before it got better. My personal life wasn't in any better shape. My dreams were dying one by one, and all I could do was focus on getting through. It was survival. Ever been there? I am sure you have.

As the New Year kicked off, my dad asked me, "Alicia, what do you want for this year?" As I sat solemnly in the passenger seat of his vehicle with an emotionless face, I stared out the window and replied, "To just make it." That was all I knew how to say, and that was about as much hope as I could muster. As much as it hurt to see my childhood dream for my career begin to fall flat and the relationship that I thought would lead to marriage go up in smoke, I also realized on top of that that I was slowly becoming a shell of a person. I was alive, but I wasn't living.

It was about that time that I began to sing John Waller's song "Something Big" as my anthem and prayer. Listen to it. It will bless you; I promise. I sang and sang that song at the top of my lungs. It stirred hope in me for the first time in a long time! I honestly didn't care what God did. I just needed Him to do something because I was desperate for more. Not more stuff but more depth. More progress. More fullness. More life. Even more of Him. Even though that was my heart's desire, I had never felt more empty or lost.

Who would I be if I wasn't Alicia Knecht, marine and aquatic biologist?

Who would I be if I wasn't going to be "Mrs. So and So?"

Who am I? Where was my life going? Everything I had dreamed and planned for was suddenly no longer feasible. Truthfully, I didn't fit that mold anyway. (You know, square peg, round hole.) Those questions are why God shook up my world. He desired to teach me who I was if I had none of the titles or accolades. He wanted me to understand my future was in Him even when I was nothing I had thought I wanted to be. He wanted me to know He still had a plan even when I had not a single one. (Oh, and for us type-A personalities, this is no good, is it?) I have since learned that making plans isn't always fruitful, and I never had control of them anyway, but seriously, a girl can dream, right?

God was stripping me of everything that was no longer necessary. That process was painful, but the outcome was beautiful, which I hope you see through the story penned on the following pages. It was time for me, as a Daughter of the King, to finally know who I was in Jesus instead of being defined by this world or my circumstances. (It is time for you too!) I must digress for a quick minute, though, before we move on.

Before moving to Florida to chase my childhood dream, I had rededicated my life to Christ after a few years of being lost and living deep in sin. Shortly after I rededicated my life, I began reading my Bible. I didn't know what to read. I would randomly pick a verse or chapter and read it nightly before I fell asleep, and those nights that I did, God would give me dreams of dolphins and the ocean. I had forgotten about my childhood dream of oceanography and marine biology, but He hadn't. Isn't that comforting? It seemed like such an odd dream as a kid because I grew up where we say, "There is more than corn in Indiana." Yes, indeed. There are cows and wide-open land. There are no dolphins! I didn't have plans to move to Florida at this time, but through those dreams, God was calling and laying the foundation for a wild and wonderful adventure.

Indiana is my roots.
Florida was my wilderness. (More on that later.)
Texas was my promise-land. (We will get there.)

As I was preparing to move, my dad gifted me, *The Dream Giver* by Bruce Wilkinson. There is this portion of the story that talks about giving your dream ("feather") back to God, and I distinctively remember thinking, "God, I don't know if I will be able to do that. I love my dream and have since I was a kid." I am sure God laughed a little because He could see the end from the beginning and already knew that that day would surely come. Much to my surprise, that day did arrive. I was ready and practically begged God to take this dream from my shaking yet surrendered hands.

My heart was broken.

I was lost.

My world appeared shattered.

Yet, for the first time, I also felt a glimmer of possibility.

Little did I know how adventurous this would become, and belting that "Something Big" anthem at the top of my lungs would be the prayer God answered and answered radically. Had I known, I might not have sung as loud, but it was and is all worth it.

I have been healed.

I have seen miracles.

I have grown.

I have been set free.

I have had new dreams come true.

I found the person within that God always dreamed I would be.

I have more faith and know God in ways I wouldn't have had I decided to stay.

It is an ever-winding road, but we serve a big God, who has big plans, and they are oh...so...good. Now that you are up to speed, *sojourner*, let the fairytale begin!

CHAPTER 2

Have You Ever...
Been Surrounded
by Darkness?

Ordinary started to feel that his Dream was finally accomplished, the Dream Giver said, "Let me show you more."
—Bruce Wilkinson

Remember how I mentioned my career wasn't going so well? We will begin our adventure there. I was a biologist for a State agency in Florida, and let me say, I only got the job by the grace of God. I walked out of that interview and told my parents, "Well, I don't think I am going to get that job. That was terrible!" However, a couple of days later, I received a call that said they had given me the position. That should have tipped me off right away. God was up to something, but I was too shocked and excited to be aware of that.

I loved that job with my whole heart. It was a dream, but underlying issues were happening long before I arrived that I didn't know would land on me at some point. I remember praying and saying, "Oh, Lord, please don't let this happen. I wanted to stay here forever." I knew if things changed and I went down this road of confrontation, there would be no way I could stay. You know those changes that occur, and there is no going back? That was this kind of fork in the road.

God was using a challenging situation to close the door to my dream, and that was hard for me. But if you have walked with God long enough, He sometimes leads us to a situation where we feel backed into a corner, and we must go through it. There is no path around. Those times can be difficult because it is hard to see the good. We feel trapped. We tend to focus on the pressure of the situation and sadness or the unwanted changes, but, in the long run, God is setting us up for something much bigger. This was an Esther moment in my life. Albeit less dire, but the pressure was mounting, and the face-off was inevitable.

The time had come to know and speak the truth, and that led to a solid five years of unquestionably tough days. The stress was excruciating. I couldn't sleep, and the only way I could fall asleep was to listen to worship music or sermons. The fear and anxiety wrapped around me every minute of every day because I was on edge, waiting for the next dramatic and ridiculous shoe to drop. Even my cat, Freya, could feel the pain! She began cleaning herself obsessively. So much so that she lost her hair! That was a sight to behold, poor girl! All of us women know what it is like to have a bad hair day, amen? It qualified.

My life was stormy, and it seemed I was trapped and swirling in a tornado that wouldn't slow down. I regularly had to "phone a friend" to ask if I was losing my mind because it felt like I was living in the twilight zone. Have you ever felt like that? When the responses of those around you aren't common sense, and circumstances seem ludicrous? For me, that is when I know there are mysterious yet significant undercurrents clashing beneath the surface and playing out in the theater of my life.

It was a battle, both spiritual and physical, but I learned for the first time how to pray scripture and stand on the Word of God. I carried Bible verses that I had written on index cards in my pocket every day. They were my lifeline because there were days I couldn't even pray. All I could do was read them or stare at them wide-eyed, if I am honest. While watching this dream die before my very eyes, I cried out to God, asking for something to hold on to. Anything. Ever been that desperate?

That was when I began to write. God gave me several ideas for children's books centered around the dream

He had placed in my heart from the beginning—nature, the ocean, and ocean animals. I sat on the back porch of my home many nights listening to the peaceful sway of the palm trees, writing, and drawing illustrations. (You guys, I am not even an artist!) That is how my first Christian children's book was born—*Sparky and Millie's Ocean Adventure*. Without my family, dear friends, and prayer warriors cheering me on, that book likely would not have happened. I didn't see myself as an author. I didn't see myself as anything at that moment, but God sent people that did. (Thank God!) Don't you love it when He sends people to encourage you? Maybe you have even been the one He sent! Those people are gifts that God sprinkles among the tension, action, climaxes, devastations, and happily ever afters of our lives to nudge us one step closer to the fullness He has for us. They make all the difference. I firmly believe that.

This writing was part of the healing process, as my original dream fell further and further away. To create, draw, write, and dream up characters and plots for my beloved sea creatures allowed me to fall back in love with such a vital part of how He created me. I am thankful for that because I could have lost it with the career, and my heart could have become jaded, angry, and hardened. I am not going to tell you I didn't feel those emotions and then some. I am human, but I loved my career because I saw God in nature, and I felt close to

Him there. The main draw had always been Jesus, even if I didn't understand that as a child. To lose that would have been to lose a part of my relationship with the Lord, and instead, He brought beauty from ashes and a children's book that combined two things I love—Him and the ocean. (Specifically, sea turtles. They are my favorite, and I loved hanging with them on the beach each summer!)

During this time, a publishing company offered me a contract, and shortly after the Lord released me from my job with the State, the book was officially for sale. It may have been the ending of one dream, but a brand new one came true! Won't God do it! He also taught me the difference during this season between a calling and a career. I had a job in my field, and in His graciousness, that childhood dream came true, but it wasn't my forever future. He had more for me, and He has more for you too!

Are you in a time where life seems to be swirling and dark? Are you feeling hopeless? Oh, I know how awful and life-sucking that can be. It feels like it will never end. Friend, I promise you, it will. I promise God is working in it. He is bringing bounty and treasures through what seems lost and the dreams that have died. You will not come out empty-handed! He also has an uncanny knack for repackaging, remaking, and bringing those lost things to life in endless ways. He can (and will) do what you never even thought of! You'll see.

What hope is He showing you right now? Maybe through a friend, a song, a new dream, or a project? He is the most generous giver of hope, especially when the odds seem to be not in your favor. Don't stop looking and believing Him for it!

Even in the darkness, God was speaking. I started having dreams and visions more frequently, and I began to connect them to God speaking. You would think that would be obvious, but remember, I am a blonde! I had dreamed for a long time and saw specific images but didn't understand and hadn't intently focused on those facets of my walk with God.

He got my attention one night because I had a dream of my future wedding. I didn't recognize the guy I was marrying, but I had never felt a love like that. It was heavenly and blanketed the entire dream. A love only God could give. The love and atmosphere of the dream were peaceful, pure, joyful, and bursting with light. I woke up the next morning, stunned because I could still feel the love heavily upon me. It lasted for days.

I wanted to keep this newfound revelation to myself, but as the Lord would have it, that wasn't going to be an option! I was in a boat in the middle of the lake the following day when a friend called, "Hey! I had a dream last night of you getting married." That will make you shut the engine off real fast! I felt like Peter in the Bible, full of faith, wanting to jump out of the boat and walk on water! It was a "God Wink" (as my dad likes to call it), especially with the loss of my dream of being "Mrs. So and So."

As you can probably imagine, there was much pain surrounding that circumstance. Even so, I muddled through that loss and started my journey to renewal and healing that included declaring, "God, You pick him. I clearly can't. I only want the one You have for me. I want a kingdom man. One after God's own heart who loves You with every fiber of his being and wants to live a big mission as a family for You. Until You bring Him, it is just me and You, Lord." God was stirring my heart with hope. The hope that one day, I will still have those desires of my heart. The pain was great, and the brokenness overwhelming. However, as my heart was buried under those ashes, hope lay smoldering, providing evidence that my heart flickered with the essence of life.

Side note for the single ladies reading this. There is a vast difference between a Christian guy and a man who is living for Christ. I didn't know that then. I was a baby Christian who was in the process of healing from my past. I thought, as a Christian girl, you go to church, join a Bible study, and date a guy from there. Well, I admit that was astronomically better than my past strategies, so I gave myself some grace (give yourself the same).

However, there should be fruit (Galatians 5:22–23, NLT) and consistency in his life long before you enter it! (And no fake or rotten fruit! Can I get an amen?) Fruit and growth from being in a relationship with God paint a much better picture of the truth than words or promises. Also, in terms of marriage, I can attest that God hadn't given His blessing to that union. I thought if I loved more or were a better Christian, it would change our relationship's dynamic, but one of the prominent issues was that there was no kingdom mandate.

Just two kids and the worldly ideals of what a relationship and marriage should be (with an immature rooting in Jesus) while being wise in our own eyes. No vision. No real purpose outside of ourselves and selfish desires. As traumatic as this experience was, God was not going to let the absence of a kingdom purpose slide. Marriage is a picture of Christ as the Groom to His Bride, the Church (Ephesians 5:21–33, NLT). There is a love that should be evident that reflects that and a mandate more remarkable than two people. I am a big believer that when God joins two (individually complete) people together in the covenant of marriage, there will be a grander purpose, and they will accomplish more for His glory together than each individual could alone. There is no judgment in any of the above, just a whole lot of growth in the Lord to recognize where this relationship fell short. (Sometimes, we don't know what we don't know. No one is to blame. It is part of the process.)

Your marriage's unique purpose will unite your gifts together to showcase a beautiful display of God and further the Biblical mandates found in scripture (Matthew 19:4–6, Genesis 1:27–28, Ephesians 5:21-33, Matthew 28:16–20, NIV). Before you walk down that glorious aisle to be united, please seek the Lord for your kingdom mandate as a couple. (I wish I had had that wisdom and direction all those years ago.) I can promise the plans God has for you both will exceed the surface level trappings of what this world considers to be marriage and life. There is a greater fairytale being written through your wedding day—one that heralds heaven and our awesome God! If you are already married, it is not too late! Turn to the Lord and allow Him to guide you and your family to that purpose. Above all else, whether single or married, make Him your ultimate purpose, and everything else will fall into place! Okay, back to the story!

Is there a promise God has given you in your dark time? Hold tight to that gift to help you through! God is a comforter. He is a dreamer. He still speaks, and even though I am not married yet, I won't forget that moment, the dream, or how I felt, and I have no doubt God will do it. The Bible says that He is not a man that He should lie (Numbers 23:19, NLT)!

During this time, I had another dream, and I think it will help prepare you for what is ahead in your journey. One night in my dream, the windows of heaven opened, and a glittery, watery substance was poured onto me. Instantly, I knew it was God pouring out a new power for my life and the days to come. The darkness and original dream had ended, and a new adventure was ahead. He equips us as He leads us forward into the unknown, and that is where I went. If you are standing in a pile of ashes, stretching to see beyond the horizon, and bravely walking into the uncertain today, stay hopeful, let Him dream new dreams for you, and lean in for the equipping!

Verses to Declare:

So humble yourselves under the mighty power of God, and at the right time, he will lift you up in honor. Give all your worries and cares to God, for he cares about you.

1 Peter 5:6–7 (NLT)

Remember your promise to me; it is my only hope. Your promise revives me; it comforts me in all my troubles.

Psalm 119:49–50 (NLT)

I love you, Lord; you are my strength. The Lord is my rock, my fortress, and my savior; my God is my rock, in whom I find protection. He is my shield, the power that saves me, and my place of safety. I called on the Lord, who is worthy of praise, and he saved me from my enemies...You light a lamp for me. The Lord, my God, lights up my darkness. You have given me your shield of victory. Your right hand supports me; your help has made me great. You have made a wide path for my feet to keep them from slipping.

Psalm 18:1–3, 28, 35–36 (NLT)

In the last days, God says, I will pour out my Spirit on all people. Your sons and daughters will prophesy, your young men will see visions; your old men will dream dreams.

Acts 2:17 (NIV)

Prayer:

Dear Heavenly Father, I love You. You dream the most incredible dreams of my life and have been dreaming about me before time began. It is hard, Lord, to let go of what I thought would be, but I trust You. I ask for new hope, purpose, and dreams to flood my life today. Show me more, Lord. In the darkness and ashes, I hear You calling me! You are lighting up my life with Your Word and promises. May I hold tightly to them! I declare the darkness is not my portion, for You call me to live in the light! I place my hand in Yours today and ask that You lead me forward into the dreams You have for my life. I release the previous dream to receive the new—trusting in Your sovereignty and goodness! I declare and decree You are lifting me up, and Your help is making me great. You hold me in Your righteous right hand, and I am secure in Jesus' name!

Pour out Your Spirit, power, love, and anointing upon my life, Lord Jesus, so that I can walk assuredly in all You have for me and be useful for Your glory. Lord, please increase my understanding of the Holy Spirit and break all barriers that keep me from experiencing the fullness of the Spirit. Fill me up to overflow. I want to know You more deeply and see and hear You in every aspect of my life. May I walk in tune with You and never put You or the Holy Spirit in a box. I lay down my will and cares before You. You are my Groom, Hope, and Ultimate Author of Dreams. You have great plans for me and a great love to experience and live out on the face of this planet! Please continue to prepare me to run into the great unknown with You. I give You all glory, honor, and praise for what is ahead and the blessings and gifts that will overflow as I live fully alive in You—a fairytale of a different variety and an adventure that shouts the prominence of heaven! In Jesus' name, Amen!

CHAPTER 3

Have You Ever... Felt Far from God?

Whatever you do, do not turn away from the faith!
—Beth Moore

Relationships impact our lives on so many levels, and I think that is one reason why God is adamant about them. He knows the damage the wrong ones can have on our hearts, souls, and destiny. However, the right relationships propel you forward, give you the freedom to be all God created you to be, and cheer you on. They are never toxic. They are never hateful. They don't have an ill-meaning agenda. They see the good in you, spur you on toward holiness, and call out the gifts and abilities that even you don't believe you possess. One type hinders, and the other one flourishes. Unfortunately, this next story isn't one that represents the latter.

After the turmoil and darkness, I had many broken pieces to pick up, and I didn't do that very well. I stuck close to God, but I wasn't vigilant about the relationship area of my life. I let my guard down. I got bored. (Does anyone else get into trouble when they are bored or antsy?) I have to guard vigorously against that because the enemy knows how to distract me in those times, even with good things but that I have no business doing. In all transparency, had this person been anyone else, I would have never allowed him into my life because I would have seen the red flags from the beginning, but he was familiar. He was a "good distraction." (Good is exceptionally relative in this case!) I wasn't interested in a relationship per se because I had already made a pact with God about it being only Him and me, but a distraction was appealing to dull the pain of healing and loss. Oh, and he also wanted to know more about the Lord, so I thought I could help.

Ladies and gentlemen, sound the alarm! Oh, you know it! All the warning bells should have been going off, and flags should have been waving frantically in every direction. Ironically, I was doing a Bible study during that time, and the material was about bad friendships and relationships. I remember thinking, not out of pride but genuine curiosity and some naïveté because it seemed evident in the study, "How does that happen to someone who is walking closely with God?" as I walked headfirst into my very own.

God's grace astounds me. It is the only reason I am still upright, but He allowed that situation to unfold to teach me a valuable lesson. Disobedience is costly. The enemy is real, and he comes to kill, steal, and destroy by any means necessary. Thankfully, light exposes darkness, and that friendship was gone as quickly as it had started, but not without some harsh realizations. Remember, in the first chapter, I mentioned giving my life back to Christ after living in a great deal of sin? A lot of my rebellion and being far from God had roots in inappropriate and impure relationships. One of my prayers, when I re-dedicated my life to Christ, was that He would make me pure. I didn't deserve it, but I desperately craved it. My heart couldn't stand to imagine a life without being restored to pureness.

During this encounter, I was re-exposed to my past, and although God protected me from the intent behind this friendship, it hit me to the core because God had done a deep work in my life. I was no longer conscious someone would go to such great lengths to be that sinister and hurtful. I had forgotten that kind of depravity, and that knife cut through my soul like nothing I had experienced before. Just as the shock and regret seeped over me, a vast chasm broke open and seemed to separate the Lord and me.

I don't know if you have ever felt like God left you, but it is an awful feeling. I cried and cried and cried.

My soul mourned. I knew I had been disobedient and although the intentions of the other individual weren't my fault, allowing him into my life was.

Months went by, and I continued to seek God, but I couldn't seem to get ahold of Him. I would watch sermons and hear the name of Jesus, and I thought, *I should know who that is, but I don't.* I literally couldn't comprehend or receive His name. That is how far away and great the distance was between God and me.

Throughout that time, it became clear that God had one question for me: *"Are you done doing those old things I set you free from? You know what I have promised you, and if you continue down this same road in relationships, the life you are experiencing right now is the one you will have. You will not have my blessings and plan for your life. You will forfeit your destiny. Those choices that reflect your past—that's not you anymore."*

Ouch. That seems harsh, but He spoke out of love. If I wanted all God had for me, I couldn't keep making these types of decisions even if, deep down, a part of me meant well. I want everyone to know Jesus! I am sure you do too! But we must have discernment about relationships, and this was one that should have been off-limits for me! Not everyone is our assignment. We cannot afford to be blind in this area, and I say that with love and grace and as someone who has tripped many times and fell flat on her face!

The life I was experiencing was void and sorrowful. I have heard pastors preach on hell, and some describe it as a life apart from God. That was how I felt, and it was terrifying. But let me tell you something positive about that experience. The fear of God was heavily impressed upon me, like an alarm blaring emphatically through my soul. It became a firm boundary reminding me to never make a move without His permission. Not out of coercion but devotion, and because there was no way I wanted to live like that again! (Lesson learned!) It also gave me a new appreciation and compassion for those who didn't know Christ personally, had no revelation of His presence, and couldn't seem to understand the power of His name. As a believer, that seems in-fathomable. I had such an awareness of the lack of God's presence. It broke my heart for myself, every unsaved person, and prodigals on the run. They lacked knowing God's love, missing out on the best life. His presence and love are everything, aren't they?

Sometimes drastic moments are necessary for us to sincerely recognize where we are still missing the mark. We will never be perfect on this side of heaven, but there are things that we must graduate from to receive God's best. That was this kind of moment where a line was drawn in the sand. I didn't want to disappoint Him like that again or live one day without Him! His mercy, grace, and love made me want to do better and be better, not out of self or works, but out of love for Him and through His power.

If you feel far from God, whether from your actions or it is merely a season, keep running toward Him. Lay down what no longer defines and suites you. Take off the old rags and dress as royalty because you are! You are a princess of the Most High God! Don't let Satan win and keep you bound by the shame of your mistakes. God is right there. He hasn't left you. (Anyone else letting out a big sigh of relief right now?) His love is as deep as the deepest sea, and His heart is for you. He chastises those He loves (Hebrews 12:6, NKJV). It is challenging to endure sometimes, but He cares too much to allow you to squander your destiny and this one precious life He gave you. It is essential for you and the kingdom. He wants you to live the life He dreams for you, becoming more like Him in the process.

I may have felt far from God, but I wasn't going to stop pursuing Him. I watched a popular ministry online during this season. I couldn't get enough of the sermons and Bible teaching. I was hungry, even though my mind struggled to compute the material. The sermons and pouring His truth into my mind and soul were everything to me because I wanted God with all my heart, and I also wasn't going to let the enemy take from me any longer. If I could stay close to the Word of God, and if I could keep reaching for Him, maybe I would be able to touch Him.

There is a story in the Bible about a woman who had a blood issue. She was so desperate that she pushed her way through the crowd. The account in Luke goes, "She touched the fringe of his robe and immediately, the bleeding stopped" (8:43–48, NLT). Have you ever been that in need of Jesus that no matter what it took, you were going to reach for Him and believe that He would do whatever you asked or had the faith for? Her faith healed her. Looking back and without even being aware, that was my mindset. If I could keep pressing in, one day, that encounter would happen, and I would be okay. One touch. One encounter with Jesus. That is all it takes! Don't think for one minute, God can't or won't do the same for you!

God brought me back from that incident fully restored. No matter how far you have fallen, there is no distance too great for Him to reach you! God began to open my eyes and ears to the things of heaven. From sorrow and distance to seeing specks of light all around me, I was delighted that God was revealing Himself to me again. It had never felt so good. I kept saying, "I can see! I can see!" There was finally light and life bursting forth as the chasm between us was repaired.

The more I watched that ministry online, the more I felt God saying, *"This is home for you. San Antonio, Texas is home."* I thought that was preposterous since I had no idea what an aquatic biologist would do in San Antonio, and I had never visited the town! Honestly, I had to look on a map to see where the city was! Over time, I dubbed it my promise-land and began to believe and stand upon that promise.

Are you ready for a funny story? I am obliged to share because you will need to know it later! One afternoon, I watched an episode of a talk show this ministry produced, and three guys were discussing relationships. (Oh, the irony!) I felt terrible for this one young gentleman because they were razzing him about being single while trying to get his opinion on what singleness was like as a Christian guy. As I sat there, folding my laundry on this ordinary day, I said out loud, "Wouldn't that be funny if he was my husband?" Wait until you see this story come back around. I'll tell you what, God is funny, and He forgets nothing (except our confessed sin, praise God)!

For the girl who once thought she had found her path and ideal life plan, God was saying, *"I have something better."* And so, the next big adventure began.

Verses to Declare:

And I am convinced that nothing can ever separate us from God's love. Neither death nor life, neither angels nor demons, neither our fears for today nor our worries about tomorrow—not even the powers of hell can separate us from God's love. No power in the sky above or in the earth below—indeed, nothing in all creation will ever be able to separate us from the love of God that is revealed in Christ Jesus our Lord.

Romans 8:38–39 (NLT)

The Lord is compassionate and merciful, slow to get angry and filled with unfailing love. He will not constantly accuse us nor remain angry forever. He does not punish us for all our sins; he does not deal harshly with us, as we deserve. For his unfailing love toward those who fear him is as great as the height of the heavens above the earth. He has removed our sins as far from us as the east is from the west.

Psalm 103:8–12 (NLT)

See what great love the Father has lavished on us, that we should be called children of God! And that is what we are!

1 John 3:1 (NIV)

God is there.

Yahweh Shammah, Ezekiel 48:35 (MSG)

Purify me from my sins, and I will be clean; wash me, and I will be whiter than snow. Oh, give me back my joy again; you have broken me—now let me rejoice. Don't keep looking at my sins. Remove the stain of guilt. Create in me a clean heart, O God. Renew a loyal spirit within me.

Psalm 51:7–10 (NLT)

Today I have given you the choice between life and death, between blessings and curses. Now I call on heaven and earth to witness the choice you make. Oh, that you would choose life, so that you and your descendants might live!"

Deuteronomy 30:19 (NLT)

But you are a chosen people, a royal priesthood, a holy nation, God's special possession, that you may declare the praises of him who called you out of darkness into his wonderful light.

1 Peter 2:9 (NIV)

Prayer:

Heavenly Father, I am humbled by Your grace. I do not deserve it, but that is what makes Your love and mercy so great. Please create in me a clean heart, O God, and renew a right spirit within me. Forgive me for my sins and wrong turns and make Yourself known to me again! Purify me so I will be clean and wash me white as snow. Yes, Lord! I receive it! With all of my faith, I am pressing in for a life-changing encounter with You.

Lord, today, I choose life. I choose You and Your ways. May all of heaven witness my decision today! I want to live a miraculous, heaven-sent fairytale. I don't want to miss a minute of it by remaining who I once was and making decisions from my old self's reference point. As I grow with You, please give me the wisdom to protect my heart and set boundaries that reflect Your truth. Reign in my heart forever as my King!

Thank you for pursuing me and never giving up on me. That even if I feel far from You, You are right here. Your Word says nothing can separate me from Your love. Nothing! You are my protector and rescuer. Your unfailing love and faithfulness stand forever! Thank you for restoring me to You, for You are life! I declare, today, I am wholly Yours—forgiven, made new, forever chosen, royalty, and Your special possession. Lord, I am putting on my royal garments and am choosing to walk in my true identity as Your Daughter and princess. In Jesus' mighty and matchless name, I pray, Amen!

CHAPTER 4

Have You Ever... Taken a Wild Risk?

Don't chase your dreams. Chase Jesus with your whole heart. In Him, the best dreams come to fruition!

It is at this very moment that I wish we were sitting across from each other at the kitchen table, sharing stories, tears, and laughs at the things God has done in our lives and the peculiar roads we have traversed. We are all in this together, aren't we? Our stories may be different, but the thread God intentionally weaves through them makes us connected in ways we would never be otherwise! I love that! Think back today. What was the last risk you took because God put something on your heart that you knew looked crazy to the world, but everything in you was screaming, "I have to do this!" You were likely shaking in your boots yet also had a holy excitement running through your veins! There is nothing quite like that feeling! When you "know that you know," yet it is wild and incomprehensible to those around you! That is where we will be camping out today. If you haven't been there yet in your journey with God, that is alright. Ask Him if there is something He wants you to do, and then be ready! I believe He has these moments for all of us at some point in our lives.

During my stint in Florida (I lived there eleven and a half years), I bought a home. I didn't necessarily want to buy a home, but out of the blue, God laid that on my heart, and I started the process of purchasing one. Anyone who has ever done that knows it isn't for the faint of heart! I searched and searched with my realtor (God bless her), and I was sure that it wouldn't happen. Low and behold, God presented one that I loved, yet it was out of my price range. I kept refusing to do a walk-through because I knew I would fall in love with this little home even more. Finally, I gave in. It was perfect— a sunny, yellow, cozy cottage in the same subdivision I currently called home.

God blows my mind with His love and how perfectly He tailors His gifts for us. Without His help, my parents, and the market being low, I could have never afforded to buy a home in that zip code, yet God gave me this one and for a great price too! (Hallelujah!) Suddenly, I was the homeowner of a little yellow cottage that I made my "beach house" even though it was forty-five minutes from the beach. (Where there is a will, there is a way, right?) It became my sanctuary and a place where God dwelt with me so significantly and tenderly. Do you have a place like that? Whether it's a chair or a spot on the floor snuggled up in the corner of a special room, your car, or somewhere outdoors, those places are precious, so I hope you do!

He knew how much I would need this sanctuary with all I was bearing and what was to come. Without it, certain things wouldn't have been possible, like working from home to get a sliver of peace as well as quiet moments for me to write and heal. It was my haven and fortress from the storms raging around me. It was also in the same neighborhood as a family that welcomed me as their own. Living down the street from them made me feel safe and not so alone.

Several years later, I was sitting on my couch in the living room of that same house looking at my bookshelves when I heard in my spirit, *"Boxes. You are going to need boxes."* I was floored and couldn't fathom why I would need those with no plans to move anytime soon. I noted this prompting from the Holy Spirit but didn't rush out to get boxes. (Silly me!) A few months later, I had that same unction to pack coupled with the urgency to put my house on the market. I shared that with my parents and expressed that I needed to step forward to see what God wanted to do with my home. If nothing came of it, then that was okay too. I scheduled an appointment with my realtor and told her about my plan. Which you are probably thinking, what plan? It was a step of faith and a big one.

What you haven't been privy to yet is that the previous year I started a side business in the health and fitness industry. It was a hard right in terms of my career and not within my comfort zone. God divinely brought it into my life to not only help me with my health but as a safe place to grow as a leader and dream again. I needed that so badly! It was a bright light in the sea of darkness I had been swimming in. Plus, it helped me lose weight, gain muscle, learn proper nutrition, and go from sleeping three hours a night to eight. That alone was a miracle. I have a new depth of empathy for those who struggle with sleep. There were days I would haul a boat to the ramp, crying the entire way, only to realize that I couldn't remember driving there once I arrived. I was exhausted. It was frightening. So for anyone in that season, I pray sweet sleep over you in Jesus' name (Proverbs 3:24, NIV).

To sell my home meant I wasn't staying in Florida, and my business wasn't at a level to support me financially (eek). However, God was nudging, and I needed to see where this step of faith might lead. My realtor listed the house that same week we met and for the highest amount possible. Why not, right? (Go big or go home. Literally!)

The phone rang early on a Sunday morning, and my realtor sounded elated and shocked as she told me she had to catch me before I went to church. I asked her, "Um, do I need to pray more or praise?" She said, "Praise. If you wondered if you were supposed to do this and leave Florida, you shouldn't. In my many years in this profession, these types of offers are rare and the best you can get."

Let me tell you how big our God is and when He says move, it is best to move! He sold my house in twenty-four hours. For the highest asking price. Cash. Done. And to the sweetest lady, I might add! It gave me such peace to bless her and hand my keys over to this precious soul. God knew my heart would need that. (I should have gotten those boxes ready the first time He spoke!)

I couldn't stop shouting. I called my family and told them the news. They were shocked too, and then I said, "Can I come to Indiana since I have no home?" I laugh at that even now. Praise God for my parents, who didn't hesitate to go along with this new and unexpected plan. I face-timed my younger brother shortly after the news rolled in, and he said, "Sis, you just forever changed your life (in the best way)." Indeed, and I had no idea the magnitude of this decision at the time. Some of my friends thought I was crazy. You will leave your career when most people wait their whole lives to work in this field, sell your home and almost all your possessions, build a business, and not look for a job? Yes, and that is what happened.

I don't know what wild risk (yet calculated because we want to move in wisdom from the Lord) God has been tugging at you to take. Please take it. It isn't just for you, you know? Others need your step of faith, and sometimes God asks us to be brave and go first! One of my favorite examples of those who were encouraged and encountered God in a very real way was with my realtor. That sale increased her faith, and she got to see God move in a way she couldn't deny. For her, it was a big deal, so those wild risks, yes, God has much for you in them, but He is also helping and blessing those around you too! Take the first step even if you are scared and have to close your eyes (and possibly hold your breath)! Let our vast God show you what He can do!

It will be scary and exhilarating. I have often heard that if it isn't, then the dream or leap of faith isn't big enough. I think that is quite possibly very accurate. Those God-moves will always be bigger than us, and that is so we will rely on Him. There will be spiritual warfare, obstacles, and stretching that may make it seem like the previous was better (and safer), but if God called you out and into something new, His favor and grace are there. That is precisely where you want to be!

The instant my house hit the market and my feet touched the floor the next day, a barrage of lies overwhelmed me...

You are going to fail.

You are going to be homeless.

You are going to lose everything.

You can't do this.

It took my breath away because those were my most dreaded fears that I hadn't uttered out loud. If you hear anything of the sort, please know that isn't God. That is the enemy (Satan) and consider it a pep rally that you are on the right track! (Go you!) Keep moving forward with the Lord!

So, here I am, leaving Florida, my wilderness. I often related to the Israelites as I dwelled in the Sunshine State because feeling at home there escaped me even though I loved parts of it. I had the makings of life yet wasn't settled. The Lord had brought me to this salt-laden land to break the shackles off, heal me from those rebellious, traumatic years, and learn who God was personally and my identity in Him. Just like the Israelites, God can bring you out of Egypt, but it takes some time and being in the presence of God for Egypt to come out of you. (Can I get an amen?) Florida was one stop on the road to my promise-land, but God had to take me back to my roots first. (Take me back, take me back, dear Lord.)

That day came when I was completely free. No structure. No home. No schedule. No career. Everything I had known for the last eleven and a half years was gone, including all of my debt but one student loan. Now that last part is worth a whole lot of hallelujahs! That was a blessing only God could arrange from a home I shouldn't have been able to afford in the first place. It was just me, Freya (my cat), my car, and a few personal belongings heading to Indiana on the next leg of this fairytale.

Can I tell you that I prayed for this moment for so long? To be completely free of all that was holding me back. To start fresh and build the life of my dreams. I resembled a caged bird relentlessly flapping my wings and slamming myself into the side of the cage, trying to break free for years. Yet, in the excitement, it was simultaneously humbling and terrifying. It was the first time I was floating without an anchor, but it wouldn't be the last. You learn a lot about yourself and God when you are down to nothing. It was the first time I thought, *I only own a car? I don't have an address of my own?* I know this may seem silly to some, but if you have moved around frequently or haven't been able to keep many belongings, then you likely know that feeling. You can feel disoriented and as if you have no identity, anchor, or stability. Yes, I was going to my parent's home, but I had never been more untethered in my life. When I arrived in Florida, it was different. I had a purpose centered around college, which led to the impression of security and stability. At this unfamiliar juncture, I had nothing of the sort, and then these words from God seemed to boom from the heavens, *"I gave you your freedom. How bad do you want it?"*

A new season of my life had begun. I was holding onto a dream only I could see and waging war in the heavenlies for all God said was mine while rebuking every scheme of the enemy trying to create hurt, division, and fear. That alone seemed to be a full-time job, but it was a sweet time with the Lord and a glorious one to watch Him show up with encouragement to keep pressing on toward what He had laid on my heart.

Are your eyes locked in on a risk God is imploring you to take? Or maybe you leaped into that significant risk with God and feel discouraged, beaten-up, and it isn't quite what you thought it would be? I promise you are in good company. One habit that has helped me hold onto my purpose and bearings is writing down the blessings and "God Winks" I have seen because of my leaps of faith! There will be more than you think!

God honors our obedience and faith. Hold onto His Word, and do not give up! You may not have a single plan, but He has plenty and is aligning the pieces of your fairytale with every step you take. He will make a way where there seems to be no way bringing refreshment to sustain and revive you. Be brave and continue to fancy the possibilities because God is full of those! You will not know unless you go (keep going)!

Verses to Declare:

> Never doubt God's mighty power to work in you and accomplish all this. He will achieve infinitely more than your greatest request, your most unbelievable dream, and exceed your wildest imagination! He will outdo them all, for his miraculous power constantly energizes you. Now we offer up to God all the glorious praise that rises from every church in every generation through Jesus Christ—and all that will yet be manifest through time and eternity. Amen!
>
> Ephesians 3:20–21 (TPT)

> For we are God's masterpiece. He has created us anew in Christ Jesus, so we can do the good things he planned for us long ago.
>
> Ephesians 2:10 (NLT)

> You will succeed in whatever you choose to do, and light will shine on the road ahead of you.
>
> Job 22:28 (NLT)

For I am doing something in your own day,
something you wouldn't believe even if someone told you about it.

Habakkuk 1:5 (NLT)

O God, you are my God; I earnestly search for
you. My soul thirsts for you; my whole body
longs for you in this parched and weary land
where there is no water. I have seen you in
your sanctuary and gazed upon your power
and glory. Your unfailing love is better than
life itself; how I praise you! I will praise you
as long as I live, lifting up my hands to you
in prayer. You satisfy me more than the rich-
est feast. I will praise you with songs of joy. I
lie awake thinking of you, meditating on you
through the night. Because you are my helper,
I sing for joy in the shadow of your wings. I
cling to you; your strong right hand holds me
securely.

Psalm 63:1–8 (NLT)

Prayer:

Lord God, I come before Your Throne today in gratitude and praise. You are good, and Your plans are ex-
cellent! For every leap of faith, You beckon me to take,

You have gone before me to prepare the place and give me victory! Hallelujah! If there is a leap that You are currently tugging on my heart to take, Lord, I ask for boldness and supernatural courage to step out and into the new adventure. Thank You for the prompting and nudge!

Lord, I cling to You, and in the tough spots of this journey, I ask for the Holy Spirit to revive my innermost being and that I may have eyes to see and ears to hear You and the ways You are working around me! Your acts exceed anything I can ask, think, or imagine, and Your power in me will sustain, energize, and do more than I can dream! I refuse to believe otherwise, even in the frustration and mundane! The enemy has no authority over my future or my dreams, and I will not relinquish my faith, for You are my helper. I will leap and trust You to catch me, and I will persist in Jesus' name! I declare I will walk in the good things You have planned! Do what only You can do, Lord, and make it rain down from heaven, open doors, and pour out Your favor. You are doing what I cannot even believe for yet, but I declare and decree I will succeed because all of heaven is backing me up! In Jesus' name, Amen!

HAVE YOU EVER?

The Cross

CHAPTER 5

Have You Ever... Been Asked to Travel the Narrow Path?

If you follow me on social media, you know several particulars about me. I love Jesus. I love helping people with their fitness and nutrition. I love Freya (my cat) and animals, all things outdoorsy, good music, my family, and tasty (for the most part healthy) food. You also know that my outfits rarely match, and fashion is not a gift the Good Lord blessed me with. There are days I even amaze myself at how "off" my random clothing choices can be. Recently, I threw on my favorite pair of lounge pants and was getting ready to head out the door when I stuck my hand in my pocket, only to find out that I had put my pants on inside out! Had I not tried to put my hand in my pocket, I would have been gallivanting all over town, oblivious to these faux-pas! (That's God's grace, right there!) If you see me out and about, I apologize in advance for my wardrobe but have decided to own it as part of my charm because God loves me despite my quirks and mismatched attire. (You too, ma'am, you too!) I am glad God gives comical moments where we can laugh or, in this case, laugh at ourselves because it makes life so much better.

My time in Indiana was a Jericho of sorts. I had to march around the town physically and spiritually to get those walls to fall! It wasn't what I anticipated, but God provided good gifts in the trials and valleys, and I bet you can say the same about your valley moments. Can you think of some of the good gifts He gave you in the low points of your journey? Praise Him for those today!

One of mine was this small spot on my parent's property where a large wooden cross that my dad built prominently stands. It adorns a sweet corner that overlooks our woods and two fields. Here the sun warmed my weary frame. The corn stalks waved a gentle hello, reminding me some things still remain the same. (Whew! Anyone else glad for that?) The night sky twinkled as the stars marched out to take their God-given place, and the lightning bugs frolicked far and wide with their time to shine. This spot brought the comforts of my childhood back to memory, but it also radiated transformation, praise, and prayer. Most of all, His presence fell there. It became a holy ground for me. I would sit on the rock beneath that towering cross, taking in the expanse of the land for hours while praying, praising, and being with the Lord. It was all I knew to do because every area of my life felt like an uphill battle. Yes, this is what I prayed for—freedom and building a new life—but even in blessings, there can be struggles, battles, and pain. God was growing me. He was teaching me what I was made of and holding me accountable to prove I would follow through with what I promised Him. I hadn't felt the weight of that more than in this moment.

The hurt was suffocating, from working extremely hard, being scared of failure, feeling misunderstood, unaccepted, and wondering if I had somehow made a mistake. The hurt of watching those I loved being used by the enemy, wondering when the final shoe would drop, and anticipating my loosely held together life falling apart. The pain of disappointment from friends and mentors, fighting to earn enough income to make ends meet, and not seeing what God had promised (yet). The hurt of hope. (If we are honest, hope can be painful sometimes, can't it? Yet, in those times, we need to hold even more tightly to it. Hope is powerful when placed in God. It won't disappoint, and we cannot truly live a life of faith without it.) I felt the hurt and uncomfortableness of growth and stretching for new levels in life. Until this experience, I was unaware you could feel this physically in your body, but you do! It is true spiritually as well! I think we have all felt those "growing pains" a time or two in life as God transforms and takes us through the refining process.

Even in difficulty, I watched God move and supply, and His Hand kept me going. It was on that plot of land that He comforted, taught, and held me together. One day, I sat there praying over my list of prayer requests and lamenting about a situation. He gently pointed to a small path between the two fields that bordered the parcel where I sat. The sun danced upon this narrow path as if it had its own story to tell and was inviting me into it. He softly yet definitively asked, *"Do you see that path? That is the one I am asking you to walk and trust Me. Are you still willing, even if those you love cannot follow?"*

I cried and sat completely frozen, pondering my answer and hoping He wouldn't make me give one. (Ever been there? Holding your breath and hoping you misheard Him?) That was a tough question because everything in me broke at the thought that maybe those I loved couldn't come along. That wasn't what I wanted, but God had brought me to this place for a purpose, and there was no turning back. I answered with a soft yes and a heavy heart but added, "And I trust You, Lord, that

You will let them catch up, and You will make this right."
I had to believe that.

I guess you could say I said yes out of obedience but simultaneously wanted to make a deal! (Welcome to playing "Game Show with God" like I know what is best.) I would walk that narrow path but would stand in faith that God would answer my prayer and restore time and relationships. I refused to give up. I couldn't! Although God isn't in the business of making deals per se, our faith and prayers are powerful and have the potential to change what otherwise may not. God's Word is clear on our ability to ask and receive (Matthew 7:7, John 16:24, Matthew 21:22, NLT), and there are moves of God that only occur because we asked or prayed (2 Kings 20:1–11, Genesis 18:16–33 and 19:1–29, 1 Samuel 1:1–20, NLT). God has given us those promises and put faith, hope, and tenaciousness in our spirits to make those tough decisions easier to bear. Those verses remind us that we belong to and serve a mighty God who can and has the power to rewrite reality as we currently see it. Looking back, this crossroad was partly a test. Would my actions match what I professed? I could have caved and settled to make some more comfortable, but I believe with my whole heart that God wouldn't have been able to do what I have seen Him accomplish in my life and family several years down the road.

Take heart if you feel hurt or misunderstood by those you love the most. God is a restorer. He is a redeemer. He knows your heart. He knows the relationships and circumstances that need restoration, healing, and unity. He can do it most wonderfully and miraculously, and you will see His glory explode like never before! It will come to pass because of your faithfulness but ultimately, His. Keep being obedient, praying, and believing. His Word says, "The earnest prayer of a righteous person has great power and produces wonderful results" (James 5:16, NLT). Ask God how to pray for those you love and then believe, regardless of what you may be observing with your physical eyes, that in His perfect timing and plan, He will answer.

God brought me back to my roots for many reasons: to test, develop, strengthen, set me free, and bless me. He gave me new friends I would have never met, and He made my "Hall of Shame" a "Hall of Fame." I needed that inner healing for my own self. Is there a time in your life that you consider a "Hall of Shame?" You may not be able to go back and face yours in the physical, but God can still turn it around.

My initial college years in Indiana weren't like most folks' experiences, and I incurred several deep wounds. Some were a result of my own poor decisions, and facing the place where sin defined the memories and shame abounded was a feat I didn't know if I was capable of.

But before my very eyes, God redeemed my past so that those memories and events would not have any power over me. It is one thing to go away where no one knows you and start over, but it is entirely different to come home to where everybody knows your name.

An impactful way God redeemed the steps of my former life was through my children's book. He gave me a book signing at my old college! This college wasn't Christian, so the fact they wanted me in their bookstore mystified me. (But God.) I took a picture that day of my feet walking on those campus sidewalks because documenting this moment was imperative for several reasons. One because I bawled all morning, and it took every ounce of strength and faith to get out of my car in the parking garage. Two because it helped me focus as I kept reciting, "The joy of the Lord is my strength. The joy of the Lord is my strength" (Nehemiah 8:10, NLT) under my breath lest anyone dare hear me, and I lose it altogether.

With every step, I was crushing serpents under my feet (Psalm 91:13 and Luke 10:19, NLT). With every step, I was building a testimony that made me an overcomer by the grace and power of God. With every shaky step and tear that fell, God was cleansing me and redeeming my past. With a final step, I arrived at the bookstore! There my past and present collided together to defeat any power the enemy might have thought he had to hold me captive, negate my worth, or strip me of my future. I was mentally and emotionally drained, yet I felt powerful! I had stared this giant down and lived to tell about it. The haunting of the past was just that, a dead, powerless figment that could no longer taunt me. (God made you a giant slayer too, and don't forget it!)

Before we run bravely forward into this adventure, one more event of redemption took place. I became an Upward Cheer Coach and Commissioner while I was at home to support my dad, who was also involved. There I was teaching the Bible and using my children's book as part of the devotional during halftime, and low and behold, much to my surprise, and quite frankly alarm, someone from my past that I dated had their kids present. I have never thrown prayers up to heaven faster and more fervently before a halftime show! (I was still getting the hang of facing my past. Has anyone else struggled through that process too? You are healed, but you find another giant needs to fall? The giant of meeting someone in the flesh, perhaps!) I wanted to vomit, but the Lord carried me through. I can't say I ever dreamed of that moment (who would?), and I was the least likely person they probably thought would be teaching their kids about Jesus. Much to my astonishment, though, they complimented me afterward. Relief and joy washed over me. Redemption. God is so good at it!

Be encouraged. Like I said at the beginning of this fairytale, I am just an ordinary girl, but God has done great things in my life, and He is no respecter of persons. Restoration and redemption. They are both a part of His plan for you because He loves you that much to take the "not so good things" of your life and turn them into great things! Trust Him. Prayerfully, every twist and turn of my testimony shows that you unequivocally can!

Face what is necessary to be free. Forgive—especially yourself. (That will preach, won't it?) Take a deep breath. The giants are falling. There is a sound ringing out! The sound of victory! The sound of redemption! The sound of restoration! God is lifting you above the past—hurt, guilt, shame, trauma, and memories—and stabilizing your stance. Let's go, giant slayer! There are more adventures to be had!

Verses to Declare:

> I prayed to the Lord, and he answered me. He freed me from all my fears. Those who look to him for help will be radiant with joy; no shadow of shame will darken their faces. In my desperation, I prayed, and the Lord listened; he saved me from all my troubles. For the angel of the Lord is a guard; he surrounds and defends all who fear him.

Psalm 34:4–7 (NLT)

For no word from God will ever fail.

Luke 1:37 (NIV)

Then Jesus said to his disciples, "Whoever wants to be my disciple must deny themselves, take up their cross and follow me. For whoever wants to save their life will lose it, but whoever loses their life for me will find it."

Matthew 16:24–25 (NIV)

The Lord will perfect that which concerns me; Your mercy, O Lord, endures forever; Do not forsake the works of Your hands.

Psalm 138:8 (NKJV)

I have swept away your offenses like a cloud, your sins like the morning mist. Return to me, for I have redeemed you.

Isaiah 44:22 (NIV)

The Spirit of the Lord is upon me, for he has anointed me to bring Good News to the poor. He has sent me to proclaim that captives will be released, that the blind will see, that the oppressed will be set free, and that the time of the Lord's favor has come.

Luke 4:18–19 (NLT)

"You can ask anything in my name, and I will do it, so the Son can bring glory to the Father. Yes, you can ask anything in my name, and I will do it!"

John 14:1–14 (NLT)

When I think of all this, I fall to my knees and pray to the Father, the creator of Heaven and earth. I pray that from his glorious, unlimited resources he will empower you with inner strength from his Spirit. Then Christ will make his home in your hearts as you trust him. Your roots will grow down into God's love and keep you strong. And may you have the power to understand, as all God's people should, how wide, how long, how high, and how deep his love is. May you experience the love of Christ, though it is too great to understand fully. Then you will be made complete with all fullness of life and power that comes from God.

Ephesians 3:14–19 (NLT)

They are like trees planted along a riverbank with roots that reach deep into the water.

Such trees are not bothered by the heat or worried by the long months of drought. Their leaves stay green, and they never stop producing fruit.

Jeremiah 17:8 (NLT)

I will give thanks to the Lord with my whole heart.

Psalm 111:1 (ESV)

Prayer:

Father God, I celebrate today that I am redeemed because of the blood of Jesus Christ, and every day You are redeeming my life to be in perfect alignment and harmony with Your will! I am under Your covenant— the covenant of the Cross! It affords me much, but there is also a cost. I choose today to deny myself and follow You. The Cross is a narrow path, but You are and will be entirely faithful!

Lord, please put every scattered piece of my life back into its rightful place and wash away any part of my past that continues to have power over me so that I may live, really live, and never stop producing fruit. I acknowledge the past hurt, but I will not be held captive by it! Today, I forgive those who have hurt me (insert names). I release my past and any trauma, anger, offense, bitterness, hurt, or unforgiveness. I ask that You bless my enemies, those who have come against me, and anyone who has caused me pain. I pray that if they do not know You as their Savior, they will grab ahold of Your outstretched hand to be saved. Help me to embrace Your grace and forgive myself too. Your Word says You came to set the captives free! Today, I am walking free in Jesus' name!

Lord, when I need to stand tall and strong to slay giants, give me the fortitude to stare them down. I believe I can do all things through You! The giants may come at me, but I come to them in the name of the Lord of Heaven's Armies. I declare and decree they will fall, and through the power of the Holy Spirit and by Blood of Jesus Christ, complete restoration and total victory is mine!

As I honor Your directions and follow You, I ask that You tenderly care for the desires of my heart and redeem time and circumstances. You see the cries of my heart and understand the depths of my longings. I believe that You will perfect all that concerns me, so I entrust those I love to You. Thank you for my family and loved ones and for always taking care of them. Where there is heartache and hurt, Lord, release Your healing balm of heaven over my family and me. For every wound and area of brokenness in our lives, Lord, please be our Great Physician. I pray for healing in our hearts, minds, souls, and bodies. Break all strongholds, unhealthy behavioral patterns, and generational curses in Jesus' name! Wash our bloodline clean, Lord! I declare every generational curse, sin, and pattern is canceled and stops today in the mighty and all-powerful name of Jesus! I plead the Blood of Jesus over myself and my family. The enemy cannot have us!

May we tangibly experience Your love and be drawn closer to You! I pray for a spiritual awakening in my family and that we fall more deeply in love with You. May our roots grow deep in You and Your love so that we may be complete and live from that place of fullness and power. Unify us, Lord, and raise us up to be mighty warriors for Your kingdom and on fire for You in Jesus' name! Also, Lord, save my family members who need to know You as their personal Lord and Savior. I believe You are bringing them (insert names) home! May You continue to bless, protect, and provide for my family. I declare no shame will ever darken our faces, for You are our hope of glory, and Your Word does not fail! I praise You for what is to come, and the great awe I will stand in for You do nothing halfway! My God outdoes Himself! I am forever grateful for You and cannot wait to see the goodness that is ahead! I ask all this in the name above all names, Jesus, and I believe You will do it! Amen!

CHAPTER 6

Have You Ever... Said Yes to an Adventure?

Faith is beyond reason; faith has reasons reason knows nothing of.

—A. W. Tozer

Some of you may be a little weary from the adventure so far and may be thinking, "Another one? I am not going!" I feel you. The last six years of my life have been one transition to another, and it does challenge and change you. God uses those sharp turns, perpetual upheavals, and even slow meanders on these crazy paths we travel to shape and transform us with a breadth and scope that mirrors the best of heaven if we allow Him the room to do so. We make our plans, but the Lord determines our steps (Proverbs 16:9, NLT), and He never loses His grip (paraphrased Isaiah 41:13, NLT) on us when those plans are much more than we anticipated. I believe He holds us more tightly.

Does anyone else find it fascinating that God only shows us a glimpse of what is ahead and draws us into an adventure with some degree of the desires of our hearts? I have learned over time that there is invariably more happening than meets the eye. Some may find that upsetting. It can be if we forget we belong to and are loved by a good God. He is good and only does good (Psalm 119:68, NLT). So when He beckons us forward into the unknown and only permits a quick gander of the terrain ahead, it is partly because He knows we may not go if we saw the full storyline. I confess that I probably wouldn't have either. (Can you say the same about parts of your story?) I believe that would break His heart because we would miss out on the blessings, miracles, transformation, and knowing Him differently and more deeply through the journey. He wants us to know Him intimately and become the type of person who can receive all He has set aside for us. He is fiercely in love with us like that and passionate about His plan for our lives!

It was the summer of 2016 before I was about to travel out of state when I felt a nudge from the Holy Spirit to buy pots and pans. It seems random, I concur. One thing was sure, though; I had this distinct feeling that if

I didn't purchase them before I got on the plane, I would have been disobedient. Does this sound familiar? I have good news. Unlike the boxes initiating my previous move, I listened the first time! Do you do a little happy dance when you get things right with God the first time, or is that just me? Progress. I was learning. I purchased pots and pans and went off to spread my wings in those wonder-filled skies.

September rolled around, and I had planned another trip. This time to my promise-land, San Antonio, Texas. There was this tugging on my heart to go. I gifted this trip to myself as an early birthday present and decided to maximize my time by going on an apartment search. Again, no plans to move yet, but a sense of urgency bubbled in my spirit to at least start taking action toward that promise. My business was doing better, but I wasn't in a position where I could comfortably move and sustain life's basics.

I spent the weekend driving around this unchartered land and talking with the Lord. I was even able to attend the church that I used to watch online from my Florida days! It was surreal to see how far God had brought me! My feet were on Texas soil, y'all! Even as my keyboard makes that familiar clicking sound transcribing those words onto this page, I am transported back to that moment in time and can feel the wonder! It was a dream! This new land was brimming with promise yet shrouded in mystery. It was an incredible weekend, and I won't soon forget that feeling of being home for the first time.

While I was nestled in a chair in the corner of my hotel room, listening to the rain pitter-patter against the windowpane on my final day touring Texas, I had a vision of a dark, black cloud barreling toward me. I wasn't afraid, but I could sense that something troublesome was coming. God was giving me a warning.

That dark cloud materialized faster than I expected. It happened on a Sunday afternoon shortly after my parents left for church. My dad returned home before the church service had ended, and I knew that something had broken. That was the defining moment that catapulted me to Texas permanently.

What occurred next could have only happened by the Holy Spirit. My response to the situation was calmness and grace, while peace flooded my soul. There was not an ounce of anger, fear, or panic. Although very difficult, and it seemed as if the enemy was winning, I had surprising confidence that God was using this situation to promptly move me to Texas. The remaining pieces in Indiana would somehow work themselves out. The next day I acquired an apartment and would be an official Texan as of February the first. (Yeehaw!) Just like that, everything changed.

I would not have moved on my own accord at this time because, financially, I was not where I desired to be. I had a responsible plan for how much I wanted to save and earn in my business. I also didn't want to accrue any debt. I wanted to do this "right." Funny, how what we determine is right and what God says is necessary can be at the opposite ends of the spectrum when it comes to plans. God doesn't promote irresponsibility or debt. However, sometimes more pressing assignments lie ahead, and He needs us to be in position. His ways are not ours, and we must have faith and be open to Him re-routing and divinely interrupting our well-made plans even when there are no resources to pull it off. (Or so we think. That is hard, isn't it?) I said yes to this adventure's final leg with no idea how I would sustain myself once I arrived. There was only enough income to cover the first month, but God always has a plan! When we see an epic problem, that only means epic glory isn't far behind!

One evening, before moving, I took a moment to sit on the floor in my childhood bathroom. I am not entirely sure why, but I guess I needed a time out to collect myself, and that seemed like a pretty good place. (All the mommas out there are shouting amen, I know it!) I asked God, "What do you want me to do? Apply for a job?" Clear as day, I heard Him as these words resounded throughout my spirit, "*Wait on Me. I am bringing it to you.*" I replied, "Okay." I wrote that down in my journal and took it to the bank, pun intended.

Are you ready to say yes to an adventure? What has God called you to do that looks seemingly impossible? Or are you mid-adventure and staring down an insurmountable problem where you need God to intervene? Life, in general, is an adventure. We can choose to play it safe, but there is genuinely no such thing. Or we can choose to walk by faith into all God beckons us to. It will likely be more than you can handle, but it isn't more than He can. Most of my adult life has felt like that. Walking through those circumstances out of my control and more extensive than my capacity to manage has brought a deeper intimacy and trust in God. He hasn't failed me yet. He won't fail you either. Take it from someone on the other side of several large ominous mountains. We can count on God to be one step ahead of us, moving the pieces into place, aligning, and providing all we need and dream! If you follow Him into the adventure, you will never regret it, and you will see tight spaces open up into flourishing, lush gardens of goodness. Adventure is calling. Do you hear Him? To the Promised Land we go!

Verses to Declare:

"What do you mean, 'If I can'?" Jesus asked. "Anything is possible if a person believes.

Mark 9:23 (NLT)

I am convinced that my God will fully satisfy every need you have, for I have seen the abundant riches of glory revealed to me through the Anointed One, Jesus Christ!

Philippians 4:19 (TPT)

And we know that in all things God works for the good of those who love him, who have been called according to his purpose.

Romans 8:28 (NIV)

For he raised us from the dead along with Christ and seated us with him in the heavenly realms because we are united with Christ Jesus. So God can point to us in all future ages as examples of the incredible wealth of his grace and kindness toward us, as shown in all he has done for us who are united with Christ Jesus.

Ephesians 2:6–7 (NLT)

He renews my strength. He guides me along right paths, bringing honor to his name.

Psalm 23:3 (NLT)

God will make this happen, for he who calls you is faithful.

1 Thessalonians 5:24 (NLT)

Prayer:

Lord Jesus, of all the adventures I could say yes to, I say yes to Yours! Thank you for calling for me! Please put a desire for radical obedience in my heart to move when You say move and do as You say. I am excited and a little scared! I admit I am going to need Your help. This seems bigger than me, but it is not bigger than my God! I believe that nothing is impossible with You! If You said it, then it will happen, and I will have everything I need to accomplish the plans You have given me. You are even sending blessings I didn't think to pray for because You love me!

As a Daughter of God, I pray for every facet of this adventure to fulfill Your will. You have seated me in heavenly places, and I have access to everything I could ever need or desire. Today, Lord, I pull down every ounce of financial, spiritual, and relational provision necessary, knowing full well that in You, I will always have enough—more than enough. I ask for a double portion of Your anointing, and I reach up to the heavens to pull down strategies, blueprints, wisdom, and knowledge to walk this call out with grace, love, and effectiveness. I ask for supernatural insight and understanding for decisions that I need to make. May the Holy Spirit guide my every move and strengthen me.

I celebrate, today, how You are working all things out for my good and Your glory. You are the God of promises but also the God who establishes them. I praise You for every promise with my name on it and declare and decree they will come to pass for the glory and honor of Your name! Not one will be left undone. Hallelujah! I thank You in advance for what You are building in my life and for the kingdom through this adventure. Lord, wrap me in Your peace and heavenly confidence as I answer Your call to divine adventure with an emphatic, faith-filled yes! In Jesus' name, Amen!

I came for Jesus...

CHAPTER 7

Have You Ever... Felt Abandoned or Alone?

I wish I could tell you these next few chapters would be easy to read and full of hilarious commentary, but like any good fairytale, the middle seems to be the most dramatic and bleak, right? It bothers me even to say that because I am a sunshine, rainbows, and lollipop kind of person. I prefer light, laughter, and happiness like bouncing on the clouds. I bet we can all agree, though, that life isn't always rolling along in sync with that peppy beat. Even as a Son or Daughter of Christ, life won't always be easy, but it will be filled with His providence and goodness, and nothing can top that!

In some circles, they know me as sunshine. I got the personality award on my high school track team. That tells you all you need to know about my running talents, and my competitive streak is nil, so I have to say I accepted this award with giggles. I won't bother to explain my kindergarten teacher's evaluation of my propensity to have my head in the clouds and not know a stranger. Chatty Cathy probably rings a bell for you, though! As you read this, know that I am sprinkling all the sunshine and bubbly-ness I can over you and am praying the joy of the Lord takes root in the depths of your being that it may temper these heavier chapters and lift you through your burdensome times.

I landed in Texas with pretty much the same items that had accompanied me to Indiana. Freya, my car, and I arrived with some big prayers, big dreams, and bold faith because that was the entirety of what I had to hold on to and trust God to do what only He could. I often say, "I came for Jesus" because that is the truth. He alone is why my feet wandered upon this particular Texas terrain under such wild and unpredictable circumstances.

At a time when I had not felt more alone or on my own, I was holding fast to what He promised. Much of what I instantly began battling were onslaughts from the enemy to push me into emotions or mental scenarios that didn't quite depict my reality. My promise-land was quickly becoming a spiritual battleground. Was I truly abandoned? Not really. Was I alone? In some respects, yes. The enemy is the master at deception, especially when there are slivers of truth twisted and cunningly spun into the lies he is trying to weave. We must guard against falling for those ever-so-subtle injections of falsities into our fairytales, but I understand, those storylines can be hard to tune out.

The first night in my new apartment, I lay in bed listening to the wind whip around the concrete pillars on my porch. It was the most unnatural sound. The howl was filled with a screeching like that of demons on a mission to make their presence known. It was in that moment of rebuking the wind in Jesus' name and declaring that fear could not push me from my promiseland that I was increasingly aware this would be no ordinary adventure.

This was the beginning of many "firsts." The first time in my life where I didn't feel like I had my family to lean on or call home for help. It was the first time I felt it was me against the world. It was the first time a new city felt scary, and if I disappeared, no one would know and quite possibly wouldn't care. Being a stubborn and "pull yourself up by your bootstraps" person, I squared my shoulders. I set my eyes on His truth with a smile and an extra dose of courage, even though on the inside, I trembled and wondered if I wasn't about to live the lies the enemy was spewing. However deceitful, those lies can seem dreadfully real, and for all my "sunshiny-ness," the mind is where I battle some of the most formidable gloom. None of us are immune to that pit! But knowing God and learning to bask in and fight with His truth makes a world of difference.

It was God and me. (Although the appearance of a few, there is no better team!) He was going to rescue me, or I was going to sink into an abyss and fade away. I felt as though my roots were cut. Truthfully, they needed to be. Not because I wasn't supposed to be close with my family (That is what the enemy wanted! He is an expert at division, separation, and tearing down families. He knows what God can accomplish through family, especially a praying, God-fearing, and united one. He hates it.), but so I could stand in strength on my own and fully embrace this new land and season with the Lord. These situations can make us stronger for sure. However, if we do not healthily handle them, they can cause wounds, fears, and defenses to perpetuate where our realities are skewed, and we accept the lies. That could have quickly happened, especially with the spiritual warfare I was inundated with. God brought several special people alongside me to pray me through and be the voice of reason and support when I was overtaken by waves of emotion. Praise God for those souls He brings into our lives for the journey. Each one is unique for the season and total gifts that are treasured for a lifetime.

Who do you have rallying around you in prayer for your current season of life? In challenging seasons and smooth sailing ones, we need prayer warriors! Agreement matters! (Matthew 18:19–20, NIV). God knows who and what we need. It touches my heart that He cares enough to send those people who get it, remind us that what God is speaking is real, and we are not crazy! Who else besides me needs that confirmation? (I see you raising your hand!) In case you have no one else to speak this into your life, allow me. You are not alone, and you are not crazy!

These divinely appointed relationships remind me of Mary and Elizabeth's story in Luke 1:39–45 (NLT). God gave Mary her cousin, Elizabeth, to share the great news that she was carrying God's Son and had become pregnant by the Holy Spirit. That is enough to make any friend or relative question your sanity, but not Elizabeth. Instead, she confirmed and celebrated that announcement! At the very sound of Mary's voice, Elizabeth's baby (John the Baptist) leaped in her womb, and the Holy Spirit filled her. I love what the Bible says next in the New Living Translation, "Elizabeth gave a glad cry and exclaimed to Mary, 'God has blessed you above all women, and your child is blessed. Why am I so honored that the mother of my Lord should visit me? When I heard your greeting, the baby in my womb jumped for joy. You are blessed because you believed that the Lord would do what He said.'" Those are the kind of people God sends in our own stories to confirm and uplift and the kind of people we want to be and hang around—ones who honor and celebrate the acts of God!

If you are feeling that sense of abandonment, rejection, or loneliness, please know God sees you. His eyes are fixed on you, and He is your father, friend, and shepherd. He is hiding you in the shelter of His wings. You are not forgotten. You are not lost, nor can you get lost. You have a God who will move heaven and earth to get to you. He will tenderly care for you and every aspect of your heart, mind, soul, and life so that you can become whole and thrive. You are loved and never, ever alone. He is also bringing the right people and communities to help you feel that sense of belonging and confirm His truth in your life.

Hold on to the promises of the Lord. Despite all the odds, Mary did. May you continue to fully believe what He said and that He will surround you with your Elizabeths too! Be honest and transparent when God does provide those to encourage you. Isolation only makes the feelings and chatter of the enemy louder until you crumble under the weight of the unrelenting noise.

That noise and aloneness may have been loud, but God's strength and vision helped guide me through. Have you ever made a vision board or written a list of prayers down, expecting God to answer? I have done both, and I have seen God use them to knock my socks off! Throughout the beginning years of this adventure, I had the same vision board and prayer list that I was rattling the gates of heaven for God to move upon. Some of them were impossible prayers just because it was fun to dream and dream big. I believe God likes that. Pint-sized prayers, God answers those too, but I think He has a lot of fun showing off with the ones that seem ridiculous. It delights Him that your faith is big enough to ask. (Hint, hint, ask!)

At the end of every year, I wrote my "preferred future" for the New Year as if it had already come to pass, and I was living it. It was a prayer with specific words God had given me as promises. Well, I have not the faintest idea of what motivated me to write one of the items down, but I did, and it undeniably fell into the impossible and ridiculous category. I had no expectation God would take notice, let alone pull it off. Boy, was I wrong! I can hear God on His throne saying, *"Oh, she thinks that would be fun! I can do that!"* with a twinkle in His eyes. God is funny and fun. So much so I almost fell out of my chair one day. Remember when I told you that He said, *"Wait on Me. I am bringing it (provision) to you"?*

About two weeks after settling in from the move to Texas, God brought me a new level of success in my business that I had been working toward the entire previous year! It was indeed a blessing and a move of God because I couldn't track my progress until the last minute during that pay period to know if I succeeded. I was flying blind, but God came through. With that success, He put a seal on my time in Indiana. The King's finality stamped everything I worked toward to remind me that my hard work was a part of His plan and not in vain but also to reassure me about the leap of faith I had taken. On the flip side, it was bittersweet because the cost of those months in Indiana seemed tremendous. I cried like a baby when that achievement became official because the work had been arduous and gritty but to see God fulfill that promise made me beyond grateful.

Although my business was going well, the situation was fluid. I didn't know a soul in this city, which made it challenging to continue to build a business outside of social media. I decided to apply to substitute teach at a Christian school and for a few other administrative positions connected to that organization. I thought this would help me get my bearings and meet some people. What happened next is why I almost fell out of my chair! A few days later, I received a phone call from a sweet gal asking me if I wanted to work in a different department. My application had been forwarded to her for a position that wasn't visible to the public. Here is the best part, you all ready? It was the same department mentioned in my "preferred future" as the impossible and ridiculous request!

God brought it for sure. He did what only He could do, and it was a reminder that He always delivers! It was another "God Wink." A nod from heaven that I was on the right track and God was present. I had no intentions of re-entering the workforce with a full-time position, but God had more plans than I was aware of. Aren't you glad He has bigger plans for us than we have for ourselves? I am—even the ones I would not have chosen like this very next assignment.

Verses to Declare:

Mary responded, "I am the Lord's servant. May everything you have said about me come true."

Luke 1:38 (NLT)

And I will be to her (Jerusalem) a wall of fire all around, declares the Lord, and I will be the glory in her midst.

Zechariah 2:5 (ESV)

Do not, therefore, fling away your fearless confidence, for it carries a great and glorious compensation of reward.

Hebrews 10:35 (AMPC)

Go, walk through the length and breadth of the land, for I am giving it to you.

Genesis 13:17 (NIV)

God loves you and has chosen you...

1 Thessalonians 1:4 (NLT)

The boundary lines have fallen for me in pleasant places; surely I have a delightful inheritance.

Psalm 16:6 (NIV)

Prayer:

Father God, thank You for Your Son, Jesus Christ. Because of Him, I have been grafted into Your family as a co-heir with Christ. I belong. I have family. I believe that in my aloneness, You will be my everything and are working and bringing whom and what I need. May Your love surround me like a shield as Your peace rests upon me while I wait.

I choose today to look up and remember I am a Child of God. All that You have said about me is true and more real than anything my eyes may be witnessing or my heart may be feeling. I am refusing the lies of the enemy today in Jesus' name! I tear down every stronghold, take every thought captive that goes against Your truth, and I stand upon the promise that says I have the mind of Christ! I bind all dark thoughts, lies of the enemy, and the spirit of abandonment and rejection and nail them to the Cross today in the mighty name of Jesus. They are defeated and separated from me! Glory to God! I am loved, accepted, and chosen by the Everlasting God, Creator of all the earth!

Lord, instill in me the habit of running to Your Word when my mind is struggling and needs to be renewed. May everything noble, right, and true from You be showered upon me today. Set my face like a flint toward You and Your plans, give me courage and a heart filled with hope. Wherever You have placed my feet is the land You have given me. I will walk my land in Your strength and lay hold of all its treasures in Jesus' name! I declare the boundary lines have fallen in pleasant places, and I stand with a fearless confidence that I will see great and glorious rewards. You go before me, surround me by fire, and are my rear guard! Hallelujah! A special grace and Your glory are here and falling all around! I receive what You have set aside for me in this land, for I am rooted in You—perfectly placed and under Your care. I am choosing trust and big belief that You will answer my prayers—the small ones and the seemingly impossible ones, for I am Your servant! It is time to come alive and take the land! In the name above all names, Jesus, I pray. Amen!

CHAPTER 8

Have You Ever... Known There Was a Bigger Purpose?

God changes our hearts and our "want to."

—Priscilla Shirer

I am sure there have been moments in your life where you stood and looked around at the circumstance and thought, "This is bigger than me." There have also probably been times where you stood in a heap of rubble praying there was a bigger purpose. Maybe you even found yourself in a dream that comes true, thinking how much this moment blessed you and changed your life forever! Those are world-changing moments, and they can arrive in euphoric or sorrowful times. Either way, we can trust that God is working and doing something significant.

This next part of this fairytale is all of the above, and at the beginning, I could only laugh because I couldn't believe my eyes. Do you remember the show called Punk'd? It was quite popular when I was younger, but I cannot say I watched a single episode. We didn't have cable television for much of my younger years, which was a blessing I didn't understand at the time. All of you parents monitoring content and social media in these challenging days are heroes! (Insert a round of applause!) I vaguely recall this show's premise being one of setting up pranks, and I would often joke that is precisely how this portion of the story felt!

It was my first week in the new position. I wasn't there one full day before I was aware there was something bigger happening than earning extra income. Do you remember the story of the guy I saw on the ministry talk show and the random comment I made, "Wouldn't that be funny if he was my husband?" I told you that would come back around! Did I forget to mention he worked at the very place where God decided to send me? True story.

Day one of this new adventure and his name flew around like confetti strapped to heat-seeking missiles locked in and headed straight for me. People couldn't stop tossing it around, and then, of course, for some random reason (never random with God), we had to speak on the phone. As that conversation was taking place, another employee overheard and commented, "Well, that was fast!" I didn't know whether to crawl under my desk in embarrassment or laugh out loud. He wasn't in my department, but as God would have it, I got this "seat" because it gave me access to what I wouldn't have had otherwise. It seemed God plucked me out of my current life and plopped me down in the middle of a whole other storyline.

This access wasn't for personal gain. It was to pray. In fact, God made that perfectly clear by not permitting me to accept any promotions or new opportunities other than what He had initially ordained. I was in for the ride of my life—spiritually, emotionally, and physically. What I am about to share with you may be deeper than you would like to dive into. But in these deep waters, God is sometimes most evident, and we wouldn't know Him in this capacity if He didn't have us become submerged in them. You may also read this and not believe it. That is okay. Had I not walked this road, I might not either, but I promise you that God is real. Dreams, visions, assignments, prophecy, intercession are alive and well. I can also promise you so are demonic forces. I thought I knew my adversary before, but I was about to come face-to-face with him in a new manner and was never more awake in my life to the reality of him.

I don't say any of that to frighten you, but so often, we dabble in the things of Satan and call it cultural, or we think the enemy is this little red guy who runs around with a pitchfork. We have made him a character that some even dress up as. I can assure you when you find out who he really is and are witnessing his evil firsthand, you will no longer patronize him as some harmless, fictional character. Yes, his power is limited. Yes, he was and is defeated. Your enemy is by no means equal with God. God is greater and reigns. Yes, we are covered by the blood of Jesus and protected. We are victorious as Daughters of God. But we have a genuine accuser and are a target. He wants to convert God-ordained territories into his and destroy all things good and holy. He wants you to lose your faith, step away from God, and for those who don't know Jesus yet, he wants your soul. He isn't playing. This is war. Not to bring more attention to the enemy than he deserves, but if we don't understand our opponent or what is happening around us, how can we fight well?

There is a war waging in the spiritual realm every day, and sometimes we find ourselves smack dab in the middle of one that was previously unimaginable. A safe place becomes a battleground. The new property in which you live is filled with unrealistic terror and fear. A trusted friendship suddenly becomes divided. A marriage suddenly seems to be unraveling. Your children are rebelling and have gone astray. Your physical health may suddenly be attacked, or there are mysterious symptoms that cannot be diagnosed. You may struggle with thoughts or emotions you haven't previously experienced and aren't from God. Maybe you have lost the will and hunger to seek God and pray, or a temptation shows up to knock you off course. You once felt free. Now you are cloaked in heavy oppression, and it is difficult to breathe under that crushing weight. Or maybe you thought the circumstances were as simple as what you were visually seeing until God opened your spiritual eyes to see not only angels but demons too. Sometimes it is our unrepented sin, a stronghold, or an ungodly door we have opened that has given the enemy legal ground to harass and wreak havoc. (It is good to ask God if there are any of those issues in our lives when the enemy shows up. I'd rather face the sin head-on than allow the enemy an inch! Ain't nobody got time for that!) Other times, your anointing draws the attack, and you walk into a situation where your mere presence irritates the demons because you have the Holy Spirit residing in you. Maybe you are even being sifted (Luke 22:31–32, NLT). Lastly, there are some assignments and acts of obedience that provoke the enemy because he knows God's plans for you, that circumstance, or relationship are great. My fairytale encompasses much of the above. Rarely does the enemy attack from only one direction because part of his plan is to overwhelm.

We have all experienced battles and spiritual warfare that have left us feeling unprepared and ill-equipped. I bet you can name several in your life, and you may be in one right now, and it feels like the fight of your life. I know that feeling: armor up, friend. God hasn't left you in this alone. He is increasing your strength, spiritually weaponizing and purifying you, and revealing Himself afresh to make you the warrior you were designed to be. There are spiritual keys and a new authority to gain from every battle that finds its way into our lives. Don't you dare leave any of that on the battlefield! Put a stake in the ground and by the power of the Holy Spirit, let the enemy know he has met his match! Because he has if we remember who we are. (You have the same power that raised Christ from the dead living in you! (Romans 8:11, NLT)) Say this with me and with gumption, "I will not tolerate it (the enemy's schemes)!" That is one of my favorite lines!

As we continue together, it may seem as if the enemy had a hay-day and won, but trust me, he lost. He always will too, but we must stand our ground in the midst of those battles and attacks. Where have you seen the enemy try to shake, taunt, and terrorize you? What does it look like to armor up, practically to stand your ground in a spiritual battle, and take the "land" by faith? I don't want to take you too far off the beaten path of this story, but also don't leave you hanging if you could use some help. There was much I knew about spiritual warfare but also didn't truly understand—like the significance of a battle or an attack, what that might look like in real life, or what I should be doing during them. Below are some principles God taught me that helped me hold my ground and advance during this fairytale:

Pray: Begin here! Prayer keeps us connected to heaven and in sync with God. Sometimes God calls us to be silent while waging war solely through prayer because we can do more in the secret place with Him than anywhere else. This was true for me. In the physical, I wasn't to approach, defend, confront, or speak about it outside of a few trusted friendships. Whether it is praying out loud or writing in journals, choose to pray without ceasing. This is where the war is actually won! (Matthew 6:6, Jeremiah 29:12–13, 1 Thessalonians 5:16–18, NLT)

Dress Up: Dress yourself in the spiritual armor that God has bestowed on you! Familiarize yourself with Ephesians 6:10–18, NIV. Applying the principles of the armor will change your life and battles! As believers, we already have this armor, but I like to remind myself by speaking those verses in Ephesians aloud during intense times. There is something powerful about that action as if you are dressing yourself in it before you walk out the door each day. (Try it! Don't you already feel like a champion? Looking at you, flexing in the mightiness of Jesus!)

Cast Anchor in God's Word: Do whatever it takes to stay anchored in His truth. God's Word brings light and helps us understand and see what is real (Psalm 119:105, 130, NIV) and is a sure foundation that makes you unshakable when the enemy comes knocking. Draw the sword of the Spirit! Find pertinent scriptures and declare the Word of God—out loud over yourself and the situation. For example, I loved anointing my apartment's doors and windows and walking around praying scripture over the area for blessing and protection. It was also an act of inviting the Lord in and dedicating it as a place where He dwells. That same concept can be applied to any situation, space, or person!

Fine Tune Your Spiritual Senses: Ask God for spiritual eyes to see and ears to hear as well as increased discernment and understanding (2 Kings 6:17, Proverbs 20:12, Ephesians 1:18, Matthew 13:16, Matthew 10:16, Philippians 1:9–11, Psalm 119:66, NLT). This will help you pray specifically and maneuver through the battle or attack with a greater grounding than only focusing on your natural eyes' perspective. God may show us things we don't necessarily want to see, hear, or sense in order to give a greater perspective and expose the enemy. It is for our good and to help us war more effectively and usher in heaven's outcome for the situation. Eventually, in your walk of faith, you will rely on your spiritual sight more than your natural, and that gets to be a whole lot of fun! What you can't see (yet) is more relevant than what you can! Take heart! (John 16:33, NIV)

Guard Your Heart: Be intentional about actively guarding your heart. (Not closing it off. There is a difference!) Your heart is the well spring of life (Proverbs 4:23, NIV), and righteous living provides clarity to the enemy's schemes. Ask God to help you keep a clean heart and refuse to harbor unforgiveness or offense (2 Corinthians 2:10–11, NIV). Sin, in any form, clouds our judgment and places us in bondage. It is not about perfection. We are deemed righteous by the blood of Jesus Christ and our faith in Him (Romans 5:9, Philippians 3:9, NLT), but we need to pursue righteousness to experience the full benefit on this earth. Yes, there are benefits to being in Christ's righteousness and righteous living! (1 Peter 3:12, Proverbs 15:9, Genesis 6:5–22, Psalm 84:11, Psalm 34:19, Psalm 37:25, Matthew 5:8, Matthew 6:33, NLT)

Lift Your Voice and Make a Joyful Noise: Insert your best praise break! (Woot, woot!) Over the years, one way I implemented this was through my praise board. I wrote down everything on a whiteboard—even the things I may not have been thrilled about. The more we praise and thank God, the less ground the enemy has to steal our peace and joy. Praise lifts us above circumstances, brings us into His courts and closer to Him, breaks strongholds, and drives the enemy out (Philippians 4:6–7, NIV, Psalm 100:4, 2 Chronicles 20:1-24, Acts 16:16–40, NIV).

Keep the Faith: Boldly raise your shield of faith—your faith is powerful and protection! Since you know how much I love turtles, imagine a little turtle and its cute shell. Feel free to tuck yourself under that cover! Those flaming arrows of the enemy will bounce right off! (Ephesians 6:16, Hebrews 11:1, 6, Proverbs 30:5, Psalm 33:20, NLT)

Lastly, please give yourself grace. Remember your salvation, who you belong to, and what that affords you. The enemy would love for you to forget who you are in Christ. Battles aren't easy, but God's got your back! It is important to remember we fight them in His strength, not ours. You will soon see the Lord's glory and every fiery dart of the enemy diminished (paraphrased from Priscilla Shirer's *The Armor of God*). Alright, Warrior, now that you are firmly planted in the Lord, lace up your shoes and keep moving to wherever you hear Him lead! That is exactly what He asked me to do...

Several weeks into this new assignment, I sat during my lunch hour at a picnic table, praying and journaling everything I observed and sensed while asking numerous questions. Did you know it is okay to approach God and ask questions? He isn't threatened by what we don't understand or what piques our curiosity. He wants us to ask. One of my favorite Bible verses is Jeremiah 33:3 (NASB), "Call to me and I will answer you, and I will tell you great and mighty things which you do not know." Yes and amen. (I tend to take God literally. If it's in His Word and He says I can have something, then I believe it is mine.) I wanted to know! I needed to know! At the picnic table that day, I was wrestling. I kept asking God: "Are you sure? That doesn't make any sense. I know what You promised. This was supposed to be a refuge, like a harbor to rest in, yet, so far, that hasn't been the case. Now You want me to pray specifically for this gentleman who is technically a stranger?"

The prayer assignment for this gentleman was surreal, and I couldn't help but exclaim, "Oh, Lord, help my heart!" Until I moved to Texas, I had forgotten about that ordinary day when I was folding laundry and watching the ministry talk show. The Lord obviously had not. I have prayed for many people in my life, some of whom I barely knew, and I love it, but this was different. It was heavy, and every fiber of my being screamed voiceless rebuttals at the thought of going forward with it. The weightiness settled deep in my bones that nothing would be the same if I took this assignment. I kept making a list of the promises God had made and trying to figure out how this lined up. Bottom line—it didn't. Then God dropped in my spirit, *The lesser is greater.* Not because this person or situation was lesser by any means, but that God had more to reveal and accomplish for my life and this gentleman than my preconceived notions about the promises God had previously given. Those promises were not void but different than I imagined. (Has anyone else seen God fulfill a promise through unconventional means? He tends to surprise and keep us on our toes, no doubt!) With that, I knew it was God's will for this season, and I could trust Him to do greater than I could envision.

I confess that I ran to the nearest Christian bookstore to immediately purchase the Bible study called *Jonah* by Priscilla Shirer. I was scared and had never related more to Jonah in my entire life. I wanted to run away. It seemed like too much for little ol' me to undertake. There had to be someone more qualified. (Anyone? Come on, somebody!)

Have you ever had a Jonah moment in your life? I bet if we were honest, we have had more Jonah moments than we'd like to disclose. (Jonah had his reasons, and we have ours.) I was determined not to be a Jonah, but it took reigning in my fear and sense of "fight, flight, or freeze" to press in and embark upon this journey. The flight option was looking good except for the part about the whale, and I love whales, just not in that context.

I would love to hear about your "whale" experience! Did running from God make the circumstances better? Easier? It hasn't for me, but I am thankful He has never left me out there running around looking like a total fool for too long. (Can anyone else testify to that? Praise the Lord!)

I thought this request of prayer for the stranger I only knew by name would last a week, so I committed to interceding for him (whatever God brought to mind) for the next seven days. I thought, "Seven days is sufficient, right, Lord? And then it's back to business as usual." I mean, seven does indicate completion in the Bible, so I did have that at the very least going for me. (Anyone else already laughing? I am sure you are!) Although apprehensive, those seven days stirred a holy excitement that I could not deny!

Has God ever asked you to pray for someone that you didn't know? Did He give you any supernatural insight into that person? We are all called to pray. We all have gifts of the Holy Spirit that God wants to use to further His kingdom and be a blessing to this world. Through the Holy Spirit, we have the privilege of being a bridge from God to people! I am still learning to walk out this truth, but I want to encourage you that if God lays it on your heart to pray, don't hesitate. We never know what the person is going through or the destiny God has laid on their lives. Our prayers are powerful and may be the very thing that pushes them to breakthrough and victory! How awesome is it that God allows us to partner with Him to help others through prayer? I get excited just thinking about it!

God has given me the grocery store as one of my favorite places to pray for others! I cannot go into a grocery store and leave without silently praying for someone. It is the most fun to walk around blessing people with prayer, and they don't even know it! If you ever want to see me cry, you can follow me around there. I laugh about it now but remember being a complete blubbery mess as I stood staring blankly at a ketchup bottle. People probably thought I was losing my ever-loving mind as I cried for no apparent reason in the condiment aisle. (Honestly, I wondered the same thing.) Still, it was the Holy Spirit doing some of His best work right there in the middle of the grocery on an ordinary afternoon. The world might be humming along as usual, but heaven can breakthrough anytime it pleases. Even in aisle number eight.

You are walking around with miracles inside of you that the Holy Spirit wants to bring forth! You are a significant player in what God is accomplishing on this earth. Increase your faith! Release the power God has given you through prayer and armor up! It is time, precious and mighty warrior! The purpose is bigger than you know, and the Lord has brought you to this place to occupy and possess the "land." Run toward your assignment, not from it.

Verses to Declare:

Then Samuel said, "Speak, for your servant is listening."

1 Samuel 3:10 (NIV)

He does great things too marvelous to understand. He performs countless miracles.

Job 5:8–9 (NLT)

God did extraordinary miracles through Paul, so that even handkerchiefs and aprons that had touched him were taken to the sick, and their illnesses cured and the evil spirits left them.

Acts 19:11–12 (NIV)

...your kingdom come, your will be done, on earth as it is in heaven.

Matthew 6:10 (NIV)

This is the confidence we have in approaching God: that if we ask anything according to his will, he hears us.

1 John 5:14 (NIV)

You didn't choose me. I chose you. I appointed you to go and produce lasting fruit, so that the Father will give you whatever you ask for, using my name.

John 15:16 (NLT)

But if I say I'll never mention the Lord or speak in his name, his word burns in my heart like a fire. It's like a fire in my bones! I am worn out trying to hold it in! I can't do it!

Jeremiah 20:9 (NLT)

Prayer:

Lord Jesus, You are not only my God, but You are my Lord. I surrender to Your divine interruptions. Where I see interruption, You see invitation. In my humanness, I am afraid and maybe even frustrated but Lord, remind me that there is "more" in this, not just for me but for someone else. Although You are writing the most fantastic fairytale ever told about my life, this is ultimately not about me. Please change my heart toward these invitations and remove any selfishness, fear, lack of excitement, or unwillingness and forgive me for any moment that I have not been quick to do Your will. Today, I turn in my running (from You) shoes, and Lord, I ask in humility and meekness that You would keep my heart pure and open to Your assignments. I vow to listen.

Lord, armor me up and anoint me to pray as I have never done so before. Teach me how to pray Your will, stand upon Your Word, and fight the battles You call me to. May the words of my mouth and the meditation of my heart be pleasing to You, and everywhere I tread, I bring heaven to earth. May the places I stand in prayer and praise become holy ground. Lord, may I not forget that the Holy Spirit resides in me and wants to move and make You known in the lives of those You place on my path. Help me to lay down my preferences and get out of the way so You can move through me! I want to be sensitive, Lord, to every prompting of the Spirit to speak, pray and lean into what You want done. Make me ready! May Your words be like a fire shut up in my bones that I cannot contain them! Touch my lips with coals of fire that every word would be pure and straight from heaven. You are the miracle worker, and I am the vessel. I believe You want to do miracles! It is who You are! Instill in me the faith to ask and acknowledge that You will do it.

Whether or not I perceive it, You are accomplishing something extraordinary, and bigger things are happening and at stake in this assignment and battle. Give me the courage and strength to stand firm in my faith as I wage war in prayer. I declare none of this is in vain because You are in it! I am using my authority in Jesus Christ to speak and call forth what is to be that I cannot yet see in the natural! I praise You in advance for every answered prayer and the miracles you are about to do in Jesus' name, Amen!

CHAPTER 9

Have You Ever... Been Gripped by Fear?

We don't prefer to walk through pain or challenges, but, of-tentimes, it is the pain that pushes us to the promise.

Assignments from the Lord can be long or short. As I ran forward into mine, seven days of praying turned into a year and a half. Yes, you read that correctly—eighteen months filled with hours and hours of praying. There were days it seemed this was my whole world (and an incredibly good one, too, I might add). A nearby parking lot became my favorite place to intercede and pray things that only the Holy Spirit could have derived. I strolled in tears. I walked in anguish, crying out for mercy, repentance, and revival. I skipped with joy, excitement, and thrills. I worshiped with my hands held high as my voice rang out across the atmosphere. Some days I walked with a quiet resolve yet saturated peace. Other days, I paced with a fiery passion. (I am all sunshine and lollipops until a little holy fire is needed!) In those prayers and declarations to heaven, laughter also flowed. I had security call on me once. Thank God the officer knew who I was and pulled up next to me, shaking his head. We both got a good laugh at me being considered a suspicious person! (Never a dull moment when walking with God!)

I call this season "Beauty in the Black Top" because, in my lifetime, a parking lot hadn't ever been such a sweet sanctuary of God's presence. It was simply stunning as the windows of heaven opened, and His warmth, glory, and presence saturated that unlikely pebbled-filled ground. It was as if only God and I existed, and we were walking and talking in a one-of-a-kind time and space.

One evening God was gracious enough to confirm a portion of what I had been praying through a conversation with an individual. I sat quietly thinking, Does she know? There is nothing quite like that kind of awareness yet not being able to respond except with non-committal uh-huh-s and oh-s. (I am sure you are familiar with that kind of response! Polite but vague and giving it your best poker face. Mine is terrible, by the way. It was an act of God I was never called out!) This particular day she confirmed the gentleman was destined to be a preacher. It took everything in me to not shout right there. Instead, I clumsily picked myself up off the floor where I was sitting and hurried to hide in the restroom to catch my breath. (My flight response was still on point, apparently!) Although out of breath and completely taken back by this confirmation, I phoned a friend. I can guarantee that phonecall began with zero pleasantries and contained non-sensical babbling that only real friends understand! Aren't we thankful for those random calls we can make when we need to tell someone what happened?

I already knew he was to preach, but God had confirmed that revelation through someone who had no clue as to what I had been praying. It was startling and beautiful. It was one of those "Hallelujah! Are you serious, Lord?" moments! I am so thankful for those "manna" experiences as we walk into the unknown with Him accepting invitations to do what seems unlikely and impossible. That was another "God Wink," confirming my ears were hearing correctly! We all need that some days, and thankfully we serve a God who doesn't mind giving us those unforgettable encounters. I dare say He loves it!

Because of the nightmares, prophetic dreams, and visions, this confirmation was such honey for my soul, yet the fear that gripped me was something I had not experienced before. I thought I had faced fear. I had, but this was on a different level. It was entirely spiritual. Fear is rooted in the spiritual (the spirit of fear), but there are times we can point to a circumstance or person that causes a fearful reaction. It wasn't one of those times. There was nothing wrong or scary happening on the surface, but I was coming face to face with irrational and unspeakable fear in the background of daily life. Fear had been an underlying scheme of the enemy for most of my adventures. The fear of failure, success, being too much, not being enough, being rejected, losing, getting out of bed to face the day, being exposed, saying the wrong thing. The list could go on, but we know fear is a liar (or I hope you do).

One night, deep in sleep, I felt a hand grab my ankle and try to jerk me out of bed. I awoke, yelling the name of Jesus, but there was no one there. These nights were teaching me how to intercede even as I slept and dreamed but to also cry out the name of Jesus over and over, so the demons had to flee. The more I learned, the less frightening the nights were. It wasn't always dark that covered the night. Many nights were filled with His glory and dreams I never wanted to wake up from. They confirmed and gave insight into what the future held. The Lord also revealed warnings through the dreams and was teaching me how to interpret and intercede for what He showed me—the good and the bad. The bad nights, though, had me cloaked in fear. I thought I would be kidnapped, tortured, die, become ill, and lose my mind. There were days I could barely get off the floor because the fear had pinned me down so heavily that death felt like it was knocking. The pressure was closing in. It was coiling around me and squeezing the breath out of me. I wanted to scream yet couldn't muster the strength to do it. I started to feel symptoms associated with anxiety, and my hair was thinning and falling out. I remember thinking, *How is this possible?* I am healthy, my nutrition and exercise are on point, I don't feel sick per se, but my body is reacting as if I have a serious issue.

I kept rebuking and binding these schemes of the enemy and declaring God's truth because I knew none of this was from the Lord. I decided to visit the doctor to at least cross that off my due diligence list, but here is the wild part, I called the same doctor that some of the other employees used, and I couldn't get an appointment. Not because they didn't have availability but because they couldn't validate my insurance. What? We all had the same insurance. I explained repeatedly and even provided names of references. The receptionists acted as if they had never heard of them or dealt with that insurance company before. It finally dawned on me that God was trying to get my attention and speak truth into my frazzled being. I wasn't sick. There was no need to see the doctor. It was a ploy of the enemy, and God was fully aware. (Isn't it comforting that nothing the enemy does escapes God's attention?)

Another distinct moment that created a greater awareness of the spiritual realm hard at work was the day I was leaving a particular building, and I felt a demonic spirit following me. Based on the location and door that I was exiting, the Lord gave me the revelation that it was the spirit of infirmity (sickness), which explained a lot!

I don't say anything of those above statements regarding fear and illness lightly. I want you to hear my heart because I know some folks have suffered much in this world, and sickness and disease are real (although not from God). My story doesn't even compare. I can only share how this experience impacted me. I understand it may seem surreal in some respects. However, this is how my fairytale continued to unfold, and had my friends not prayed me off the floor in those moments of absolute collapse, and God's hand wasn't gripping me tightly, I am not sure what would have become of me. The enemy had come in strong, and this situation had become a full-on battle between light and dark in the spiritual realm. There were a few reasons for that:

1. As the undercover prayer assignment got deeper, the battle became more intense for freedom, healing, and destiny. When taking ground for

the kingdom of God, be prepared for battle—not against flesh and blood but evil principalities and spirits (Ephesians 6:12, NLT). Opposition and battles will be par for the course, but that doesn't mean we fight alone or succumb to fear because the battle is the Lord's! (Joshua 1:5, Jeremiah 20:11, Exodus 14:14, 2 Chronicles 20:15, NLT)

2. God is light, and light and darkness will never mix. Anytime the enemy has authority in certain circumstances, cities, organizations, or places, the light causes a reaction. The darkness desires to control and hold on to the territory currently in its possession. Light says darkness has to go, and darkness will never be happy about that! God gave me a vision one day for San Antonio, and it showed tentacles infiltrating the city (imagine a big octopus and tentacles weaving through buildings and wrapping themselves around certain areas). Each one of those tentacles represented a demonic stronghold. As God would send me into different parts of the city to run errands, etc., He had me pray for those tentacles to be cut and that He would seal this city off from evil! If God sent you into an assignment that irritates the darkness, then He has a great purpose to accomplish in that place and through you. You are called to

be salt and light, share the Gospel, heal, and set captives free! Don't conform to the pressure but stand tall and let His light shine through you! (Luke 10:17, Mark 16:15-18, Matthew 5:13–16, John 3:19–21, John 1:5, NLT)

3. This battle was concurrently a fight for my own life and future. God was allowing me to go through this boot camp to be able to lay hold of all He had for me, be sifted, take dominion over my promise-land, sharpen my spiritual prowess, walk in destiny, and provide a new depth of understanding for certain spiritual gifts. None of this happened out of punishment but because there were promises within! It was a time of purification, equipping, and testing my faith to prove it true and genuine. This was a crash course for me on spiritual warfare and intercession, and I won't soon forget the pruning of this fire. However, the results from this experience, miracles, and presence of God are some of the gifts I will never get over for the rest of my life. What the enemy meant for harm, God was using for my good! (1 Peter 1:6–7, Luke 22:31–32, Psalm 34:18–20, Psalm 144:1, Genesis 50:20, NLT)

The enemy didn't want victory in these circumstances and certainly put up a good fight, but he was defeated anyway. We rarely desire a battle, but it teaches us how to flex our spiritual "muscles" and grow! Sometimes that is what God requires to accomplish His will on this earth and for us to learn to apply our faith and graduate. During this battle and assignment, there was a lot of purifying happening in my own heart too, and my learning curve was substantial. I only have a vague understanding of why God chose me to go through this, and maybe it was partially because He knew I would say yes even though I had no idea what I was doing. (That happens often. This book would be another good example. Ha!) We choose some situations, and others seem to choose us, but His heart is for us in every facet of them.

You might be wondering the same. Why me, Lord? Why this assignment? If it is a call to intercession, then there must be an immediate need. I'd also wager the "why" has much to do with what the Lord has deposited in you and your faith in the situation. Just like in the story of David, God looked at his heart and not his outward appearance or his status in the world (1 Samuel 16:7, NIV). God knows who can handle the situation with humility and care. He also knows who will accept the challenge and is willing to fight for what matters to Him. We can rest in the fact God is infinitely wise and in total control too. Instead of seeing the assignment as a burden, see it as a privilege. A chance to do His will and bring Him glory. A chance to send Hell packing.

I am sure there are some reasons behind this assignment and the spiritual attack that I won't understand until I get to heaven. This life can be full of mystery, can't it? Even so, I believe that God has some awesome surprises in heaven for the circumstances we couldn't grasp while we roamed upon this earth, and I am excited to see and hear the stories behind our life's twists and turns! I hope by hearing my story that if you do ever walk through a time of intense fire and spiritual warfare, that you won't feel alone or allow fear to overtake you but will know the warfare is real, and there must be a lot at stake (as well as big rewards and victories!). Otherwise, God wouldn't have allowed it. Even with that being true, the spirit of fear and the associated characteristics are never from the Lord. Ever.

What does the Bible say about those facets of warfare? How do we become effective at taking authority over the principalities of darkness? I am no Bible scholar and am still learning to exercise the authority and power God has given me as a believer in Jesus Christ, but I can tell you that in those times when you feel surrounded by the demonic, we cling to the Lord. He is our haven, strong tower, a warrior that stands next to us, Prince of Peace, and we use our sword (The Word of God). We fight our battles not physically but spiritually and trust God to move mightily and swiftly on our behalf. We don't fight fair when it comes to the enemy. We take him out by declaring the Word of God unapologetically through worship, praise, prayer, and intercession. In Matthew 4:1–10 (NIV), the enemy tempted Jesus, and each time He responded to Satan with "It is written," followed by the Word of God. Whatever the battle, attack, or temptation, that is a perfect example of how we should respond, as well. The Word of God is powerful—the supreme authority in all the universe. Everything bows to His Word, and Satan doesn't stand a chance against it. What is your favorite Bible verse to do battle with? Declare it today and be assured that Who is in you and surrounding you is greater than who is against you! (1 John 4:4 and 2 Kings 6:16–17, NLT)

As I clung to the Lord and my favorite verses, I cried out regularly, "Lord, have mercy. Please do what is needed but have mercy," because of what He had allowed me to see regarding various situations and because the entire assignment was much to bear. God answered even my one-word prayers and never failed to carry me through. Whether one word or groans and tears, He hears and never hesitates to move at the sound of our cries. When we don't know what to pray, we can have comfort in this verse from Romans 8:26 (NIV): "In the same way, the Spirit helps us in our weakness. We do not know what we ought to pray for, but the Spirit himself intercedes for us through wordless groans." There were moments I was overcome by the Spirit with groans and tears and knew He was interceding when I didn't have the words. One night, while doing dishes, I grabbed the edge of my kitchen counter and doubled over as sobs broke forth and the Spirit washed over me, praying for what I didn't have the knowledge to ask for. He has come like a gentle breeze in my life and like a freight train. Both equally powerful, profound, and marvelous.

I was a bit shaky in my emotions and thoughts. On the outside, by the grace of God, I held it together most days, but on the inside, I wasn't myself. Despite all of that, I loved every minute of the new closeness with the Lord. He was so apparent in the day-to-day as well as in supernatural ways. It was as if He had me in a bubble, and as I watched the enemy parade in front of me and taunt, I was safe and surrounded by God. He even made sure I had my own office, which allowed me the freedom and solitude to pray and savor each revelation. He was immensely kind and gracious to me during this journey, and that same grace abounds toward you with whatever you may be enduring or facing.

To give you an idea of how jumpy I was and because by now, I am sure you need a good belly laugh, picture this! I was standing in the middle of a football field to admire the newly built turf. Out of nowhere, I heard this buzzing sound. It was deafening and seemed to be headed straight for me. I swung my arms, ducked, jumped, danced, and walked quickly away because I thought this enormous bumblebee was about to attack ferociously. Have you ever had something happen so fast yet feel like slow motion? I thought, "Why isn't anyone else alarmed?" Yes, there were people around. You know this type of situation—you fall and then act real calm and relaxed afterward, pretending like it didn't happen. Don't tell me you have never done that! That was me this afternoon! As it turns out, that distinct threatening sound belonged to an aerial drone. No bumblebee. (Sigh of relief! Just an overactive imagination and rattled emotions.) One can only pray they weren't videoing, and if they were, someone somewhere got a real good laugh at the blonde doing a frantic jump and dance in the middle of a football field. Had I known, I would have at the very least added a little cheerleading pizzaz to make the whole charade exceedingly worthwhile. (Gooooo me!) I laugh at that image now, but it was no laughing matter then. It was a good indicator of how on edge I was dealing with the spiritual warfare, praying, working full time, and building a business. Have you ever felt on edge? Hang on to God, and don't let go. He won't let you fall!

When God appoints certain assignments or allows battles to change and equip us, it sometimes feels as if we are alone with Him in it. There will be certain seasons for you and God alone, and they yield increases that wouldn't be possible otherwise. I would add a note of caution here—just because this was the situation God had me endure in this season, and for the most part alone, that may not be the case for you. I recommend seeking the Lord and wise counsel from someone you can trust that has a strong biblical foundation. Trust and spiritual maturity are paramount. Let the Lord guide you to the person(s) whom He has deemed appropriate. Unfortunately, no matter how well-meaning or even Christian, not everyone can handle the details of such encounters. I learned this the hard way and by accident. Although there may have been some truth in their response to my unexpected breakdown that included wailing coupled with a lengthy yet fragmented explanation, it wasn't accurate for this situation nor helpful. In that moment of vulnerability, a friend who had a similar experience overheard the conversation and quietly said, "They don't understand." I was thankful she did and shared that wisdom so that I didn't take it personally or allow the enemy to condemn and cause unfounded guilt or insecurity.

I am grateful for that painful experience because it taught me to listen attentively to the Holy Spirit, learn what to receive from others' interpretations, use wisdom when sharing, and be mindful of my own responses when someone shares their struggles or experiences. Please hear me if you have been wounded by someone's interpretation of your assignments or battles. First, release that hurt because they probably didn't understand either. Secondly, just because you're in a battle, that doesn't mean it's your fault, or you did something wrong. (I know someone needs to write that down and believe it today!)

Okay, ready for my James Bond 007 stunt? One day God prompted me with, *"Write an encouraging note to him (the one I have asked you to pray for)."* I sat on that for a few days because I didn't want to write the note, nor did I know what I was supposed to say. Plus, I liked my anonymity at this point and was afraid my cover would be blown. However, there was also this bubbling joy in my soul that I couldn't avoid. (Writing encouraging notes is my jam! God sure knows how to pick the tasks for us!)

Several days later, I was moseying through the grocery store when I haphazardly took a shortcut through the card section. I glanced at the rack of millions of cards as I breezed on by with my basket on a mission to pick up a few essential items when one jumped out at me. (Not literally! That would have been a miracle worth documenting!) Of course, the card was perfect, so I put it in my basket and carried on with my shopping. I had my favorite pineapple coconut drink in my basket, which ended up spilling onto the card, so I was obligated to buy two cards, not one! I guess the Lord thought I needed a keepsake as a reminder of what He was doing in this wild and fun plot He was weaving together. Amused, I thought, *Okay, Lord, you are making a point here*, as the scanner at the checkout went beep, beep.

The Lord ended up giving me some words to write in the card, including a verse, and I wrote it super slowly with my best penmanship in hopes it would be a good disguise. Anyone who knows me and has seen my regular handwriting can conclude that I should have been a doctor. Have you noticed our penmanship seems to worsen as we age, or is that just me? (Good grief!)

Cue The Bond Music...007 has arrived. I showed up several times later in the evening to his office building, yet to no avail; there was always someone humming about! I decided those attempts were a bust, and I would shoot for the wee morning hours. I hustled in through the door just as the dawn broke over the sky, squatted down low, ran through the wide hallway, made a split-second stop to chuck the note under the door, and then with a quick look to the left and the right to check my surroundings and still in a squat; I ran out the back door! I should have somersaulted like those guys in the movies, but I can only imagine how that would have turned out! (Grace isn't my middle name.) A deep breath followed by a few giggles exited my lungs. I couldn't believe I had done it! The note had been delivered, and hopefully, that was that. Later, I found out there were cameras in that hallway. Whether active or not, I will never know, but it certainly adds suspense to my rather comical escapade.

Do you have any 007 moments where you have done something super secretive and joy-filled for God that we should know about? (#idomyownstunts) I would love to hear them! Covert Operative of heaven, you have my permission today to relive it, let the goodness permeate your being, and enjoy that snippet of theatrics one more time. God made these moments good for the soul!

Verses to Declare:
> For God has not given us a spirit of fear, but of power and of love and of a sound mind.
>
> 2 Timothy 1:7 (NKJV)

> When the seventy-two disciples returned, they joyfully reported to him, 'Lord, even the demons obey us when we use your name!
>
> Luke 10:17 (NLT)

> Truly I tell you, whatever you bind on earth will be bound in heaven, and whatever you loose on earth will be loosed in heaven.
>
> Matthew 18:18 (NIV)

> He sends his command to the earth; his word runs swiftly.
>
> Psalm 147:15 (NIV)

You will keep in perfect peace those whose minds are steadfast, because they trust in you. The path of the righteous is level; you, the Upright One, make the way of the righteous smooth.

Isaiah 26:3, 7 (NIV)

Surely goodness and mercy shall follow me all the days of my life, and I shall dwell in the house of the Lord forever.

Psalm 23:6 (ESV)

For he will conceal me there when troubles come; he will hide me in his sanctuary. He will place me out of reach on a high rock.

Psalm 27:5 (NLT)

A happy heart is good medicine and a cheerful mind works healing, but a broken spirit dries up the bones.

Proverbs 17:22 (AMPC)

Prayer:

Dear Lord, I confess I am struggling and fearful. The fear is so great that I am overwhelmed and anguished. For all the situations where I feel under attack and am fighting a spiritual battle, I take authority as Your

Daughter and wield my sword. It is not by might, nor by power, but by the Holy Spirit that I live, wage war, and obtain victory! Your Word says You have not given me a spirit of fear but one of love, power, and a sound mind. Today, I receive that promise and declare it as truth over any area of my life where I feel the spirit of fear nipping at my heels and taking up space in my soul and mind. Please give me revelation and understanding to reveal the root of the fear so that it can be severed from my life. I command the spirit of fear to leave today in Jesus' name! Fear, you must let me go!

I bind every feeling and physical situation that is contrary to Your Word. I bind the spirits of anxiety, infirmity, oppression, heaviness, manipulation and witchcraft, death, and any other demonic spirit present. I do not receive them or their tactics, and I declare them broken off my life in Jesus' name. I am covered by the blood of Jesus, and they have no place here! I cancel every curse and attack in Jesus' holy name and serve the enemy an eviction notice today! He must flee!

Lord, I loose Your peace, joy, understanding, assurance, protection, freedom, and healing over me. You paid for it all on the Cross, and all I need to do is receive! Fill me with an unwavering faith—faith like a river flowing deep and gushing forth! I declare Your goodness and mercy are following me all the days of my life, and I will dwell with You forever. The situation may be intense, but You are my banner. I will not be intimidated or retreat! I am coming out triumphant and equipped to do more extraordinary things than these!

I praise You for the joy You are releasing into my weary soul and the laughter You are putting on my lips. Lord, add a dash of cheer to my heart too! Thank you for making my path level and smooth. Thank you for hiding me in Your sanctuary and placing me high on a rock and out of reach! Lord, You get all the glory, honor, and praise! Please visit me, both day and night, through quiet whispers, subtle impressions, glorious visions, and moves of Your mighty hand! I long to behold and be near You. Take over my dreams, Lord. Flood them with revelations and continue to teach me. May I feel Your warmth, see You all around me and walk with You closely as Your Daughter and loyal friend. I praise You for being my loving Father, great defender, gentle shepherd, and Almighty King! Thank you for Your Word, and that it doesn't return void. It is powerful and, when sent forth, accomplishes Your perfect will. I am declaring and using Your Word to shift this battle! Glory is coming and will shine so bright! In Jesus' name, Amen!

CHAPTER 10

Have You Ever... Had Love Flood Your Heart?

It is kind of fun to do the impossible.

—Walt Disney

This part of the fairytale is the one we wait for—the chivalrous romance, but it may not be what you expect. So far, we have slain giants, taken risks, gone on new adventures, been healed and set free, conquered battles being waged, turned in our running shoes, and rose as mighty warriors spiritually weaponized for more wondrous works, but this part holds a special place in my heart. I cannot think of another time in my life I have experienced such a love as I did for this individual. I know you are reading the title of this chapter and thinking, "Of course!" I have no doubt you have experienced great love in your life. I hope you have had the type of encounter with love that I am about to share with you! It is divine and will give you a greater understanding of the love of our Father. It changed my whole life and heart. The love I am talking about here isn't worldly love. We tend to "love" everything these days. But my love for chocolate and the love for the people God has blessed me with are two entirely different things! (However, sometimes pretty close, right? I'm kidding!) We get glimpses of this in those we love and those who love us, but when God gives us a love for someone (This could happen for a place or nation too!), we have not had a relationship or connection with and know very little about, it is a supernatural love.

In her Bible study *The Quest*, which I happened to do with a small group during the same time as this adventure, Beth Moore once said that there was the potential to fall in love with someone through intercessory prayer. (Boy, did I get some elbows to my ribs during that video session!) I believe that statement to be true because that is what God gave me. It was a bone-deep love and burden (the right kind) for someone that had nothing to do with my feelings, nor did I choose it. The Bible shares insight into the love mentioned above, as well as several others. There is agape, philia, storge, and eros. To give a broader understanding of these loves, let's look at those four Greek words and their general definitions from C. S. Lewis's *The Four Loves*. They are as follows:

Agape—pure, deep, self-sacrificing, unconditional, God's love

Philia—brotherly, friendship, but not camaraderie (think Jonathon and David)

Storge—family, affection

Eros—sexual, passionate (think Song of Solomon, and that is all we will say about that!)

Several of these loves can overlap to some extent and are present in different types of relationships and stories throughout the Bible. For my story, the focus is on agape love. Quite frankly, in all the turmoil, trauma, fear, anxiety, and spiritual warfare, it was shocking to think I could love in any breadth. But that is what God does. That is who God is. Everything flows from His love, and because He is living inside of us, His love flows through us even in situations we would least expect. We can't conjure this type of love up, nor can we ignore it. I believe that is when we know the love is truly from Him.

Love is sacrificial in so many aspects. Like our big dreams, there is a cost, but the investment is priceless and the return, although that is not why we love, is more significant than words can express. We love others because we were made for it through the love of our

Heavenly Father, and when God is involved, it blesses and radically changes us to be more like Him.

I recall God asking if I would say "I do" and lay down all that He had promised me so that this gentleman could have his destiny and ministry. Out of no power or capability of my own, I told God I would. There was nothing I wanted more at that moment than to be obedient and see this gentleman receive all God had said! I could have only surrendered my hopes and dreams because of God's love and the love God had put in my heart for him. Forever etched in my mind will be the day I was strolling through the parking lot, and as I slowly turned toward the north, a vision flashed before my eyes of this man standing on stage preaching to a stadium full of people. I was standing stage left facing a small set of black stairs that led to the platform as I watched him preach. As the vision disappeared, God pointed out Billy Graham as a relevant example. It was indeed the most beautiful, breathtaking, and astonishing sight. You might be asking, "Does God do that? Ask us to lay down personal promises and give visions of others?"

Sometimes, and the circumstances will be different for everyone. Recall the story in the Bible of Abraham and Isaac (Genesis 22:1–19, NLT). God asked Abraham to sacrifice his only son, the one God promised would carry on their lineage and make his descendants as numerous as the stars. Abraham trusted God's promise and headed up the mountain in obedience even though it made no sense in light of what God had previously said. God provided a ram, so Abraham didn't have to follow through, yet it proved beyond a shadow of a doubt that Abraham's heart was sold out for God alone. It also proved God's faithfulness and trustworthiness. We can always count on Him to come through and make good on His promises.

I have often wondered how Abraham had the faith and was amenable to march up the mountain and prepare to sacrifice his son. The only conclusion I can come up with is that when you know God personally and believe His promises, you will take actions and steps of faith your flesh normally would not. You understand in the depths of your heart and soul that no matter what, He won't put you to shame. I pray we pass the test like Abraham laying down whatever God requests when it comes to our lives. What about you?

Okay, so right about now, I can hear you saying, "But wait! What about the guy? Hurry up already! That is the good part!" We fancy the love and relationship storylines, don't we? Alright, alright. I will tell you. The Lord allowed me to see and declare much in prayer for him. Standing outside his office door and laying hands on it was a heavenly experience, unlike anything I had previously encountered with the Lord. The heavens opened where my feet were daintily planted full of faith as the toes of my shoes snuck up as close as possible to the threshold of his door. Timid and nervous yet never wanting to leave that tiny piece of holy ground is how I prayed some of the most prophetic and fun prayers God has ever given me the vocabulary for. God eventually orchestrated a day when reaching out to him was appropriate, and obscurity was no longer necessary. That phone call started a short time of speaking life over him and being his friend.

I was sitting at my kitchen island one evening and felt the Holy Spirit heavily upon me. I suddenly had warmth flood my body; my hands were sweating. (This is normal for me when the Spirit starts to move, but I was still getting used to it. My body and hands feel as though fire is bottled up in them!) I had a strong impression that the next day I was going to have to make "the call." I had a vision of a door cracked open but closing slowly. I was on one side, and he was on the other. Instantly, I was aware that time was short. (That was more accurate than I realized!)

The next morning, I woke up to a phone call from a dear friend asking if I had seen the Verse of the Day from a popular radio station. I had. It was "Be still and know that I am God" (Psalm 46:10, NLT). Some might interpret that to mean the call was not to be made, but my wise friend said, "I don't think that is what God is trying to tell you. He wants your soul to be still, and I have this song that came to mind. It is "Peace Be Still" by The Belonging Co.

Her words resonated in my spirit. I prayed and worshiped to that song as I rolled along on the freeway to Dallas. Ironically, what hit my heart so intensely wasn't the "peace" or "be still" lyrics in the song. It was the "faith, rise up." That was a common phrase prayed over him repeatedly long before I knew it was popular. (I am usually the last to know these things. Kind of like my fashion sense!) That phrase was confirmation, and I had to pull over at the nearest gas station because I was undone. Here I was emotionally wrecked and crying just on the outskirts of Dallas. There was a sense of urgency in my spirit that I was unable to ignore. I couldn't go a mile more without picking up the phone! Have you ever had the Holy Spirit arrest you like that? If you have, you will never be the same!

I decided to play the song one more time and listen intently to make sure I was picking up what the Lord was putting down! As I immersed myself in the lyrics, I heard the Lord say, *"He is ready."* And then, a few bars later in the song, He repeated it, *"He's ready."* For a note of clarity, I have yet to hear the audible voice of God, so when I say "hear" or "He said," it is Him speaking in my spirit as if He drops the words into my mind and heart.

As those words reverberated through my soul, my immediate response was, "Oh, Lord! What if I am not?!

I don't think I am!" Have you ever been there? Whatever the Lord has previously revealed sounds incredible until He asks you to move upon what He has shown you and said! In those moments of God calling us to action, no truer words can be sung—*faith, rise up.* God was preaching to me now. (Funny how He does that, isn't it?) The very prayer sent to the heavens on behalf of someone else was being asked of me.

I picked up my cell phone with trembling hands, still discussing the details of this with God, and I dialed the main office number where he worked. I prayed so hard that the secretary wouldn't ask me, "Who is this?" Praise God neither secretary I was patched through to uttered those fateful words. I thanked God profusely for that! Relief flooded me. Suddenly the line clicked, his distinguished voice filled the airwaves, and you would have thought we were long-lost friends.

As the conversation unfolded, he began sharing what God was doing in his life. He expressed some changes and used the same phrasing that I had prayed for him! I could have wept. I was thankful God was moving in his life and tugging on his heart! It was truly priceless! God gave me a peek of how He had been working the whole time I had been praying, and that was a gift of a lifetime.

When has the Lord allowed you to see an answer to prayer, even if it was only a quick peek? I think that happens more than we realize, and so often we aren't looking, or we dismiss it! Keep your eyes open because God longs to show you the fruit of your efforts! Whether God allows us to see or not, may we always pray with sincere faith and believe God for the impossible. It's what He does best!

Where is the gentleman now in terms of what God revealed? Well, that answer will come with time, but I am confident God is still working, and the visions and dreams will come to pass. (Oh, the suspense!) God didn't permit me to disclose everything He had shown. That season and position God placed me in were specific, and boundaries were set firmly in the place of allowing God to lead, unconditional love, and encouragement (and lots of self-control on my part!). Isn't that what we all need?

That is a teaching moment in itself. We are called to love and encourage people along in truth toward all God has for them. It is a journey for every one of us to grow in and lay hold of. Each one of us has that responsibility when God calls. It takes courage. It takes leaving things behind. It takes letting go. It takes allowing God to mold, heal, and prepare us. It requires activating faith, surrendering, and submitting. We say yes to the adventure, and the Lord guides the outcome. (That's a praise! But handing over control to God isn't easy, is it?) Regardless, we do not stop praying for what He has shown us until we see it come to fruition or the Lord removes the assignment.

And with that, the clock struck midnight, and that heavenly appointed door gently closed. God confirmed He was lifting this cherished assignment with two visions. They touched my heart deeply as I was having to let go (at least from the original intent. It has been almost five years now. I still receive dreams and visions about him and pray when God asks).

In the first vision, I quietly, with my head bowed, knelt before the Lord. He extended His scepter, placing it upon me. It was a "well done, good and faithful servant" moment as well as one signaling the completion of preparation. In every assignment God gives, He wants us to graduate into a new authority and position. That is accomplished by His grace, and it was the only reason I had made it to this point in the fairytale.

In the second vision, my heart cracked open, and water gushed through it. It wasn't plain old water, though. It had that same glittery aspect like the substance poured out in my Florida dream mentioned in earlier chapters. God was healing my heart, providing refreshment, filling me with new life, and making me whole. Did that remove the fierceness of the battle immediately? No, but those visions brought comfort and peace and reminded me that the assignment and the love flooding my heart was real and had purpose.

Is there a long-standing prayer request you have been contending with? Where does your heart need to be refreshed and restored? One of my favorite verses that I held tightly to was Romans 5:5 (NIV): "And hope does not put us to shame, because God's love has been poured out into our hearts through the Holy Spirit, who has been given to us."

I pray you claim that verse today and feel His hope and love flood every nook and cranny of your heart and soul to the very places where it seems you have run dry. His love conquers everything! He can make it as though the suffering from the battle and spiritual warfare never happened (Daniel 3:26–27, NLT). You will treasure every vision, prayer, dream, sacrifice, and your life will never be the same. I know mine sure won't, and I wouldn't change it for the world! He can also give you a brand new love for life and the people He calls you to! Even as you read this, I hope you tangibly feel a fresh outpouring of love from God for those you already have in your life and the special people He gives you a burden to call forth heaven to earth on their behalf. I pray that you get to see them and their future in the manner heaven does too! It is truly spectacular, and you will begin to want more for them than you could want for yourself!

This chapter will end differently, but I have still included some of the verses God gave me to pray and declare during this time. They became the bedrock for me, and I pray they bless you as well. I want to pass along the prayer the Lord gave me for my future marriage in this assignment. Single ladies, it is all yours! For those who are married, please feel free to edit as necessary. In both cases, take the liberty to make the prayer your own. The Holy Spirit will lead you in what to pray, and you will see the miraculous hand of God move in unique and specific ways! Oh, how that makes my heart leap with anticipation! I cannot wait to hear what the Lord does through your courageous heart to pray for those He entrusts to you! I declare over you, Daughter of the King, faith, rise up!

Verses to Declare:

And may the Lord make your love for one another and for all people grow and overflow, just as our love for you overflows.

1 Thessalonians 3:12 (NLT)

Always be joyful. Never stop praying. Be thankful in all circumstances, for this is God's will for you who belong to Christ Jesus.

1 Thessalonians 5:16–18 (NLT)

May God himself, the God of peace, sanctify you through and through...

1 Thessalonians 5:23 (NIV)

Now, because of your obedience to the truth, you have purified your very souls, and this empowers you to be full of love for your fellow believers. So express this sincere love toward one another passionately and with a pure heart.

1 Peter 1:22 (TPT)

Such love has no fear, because perfect love expels all fear.

1 John 4:18 (NLT)

Abide in my love.

John 15:9 (ESV)

But the Holy Spirit produces this kind of fruit in our lives: love, joy, peace, patience, kindness, goodness, faithfulness, gentleness, and self-control. There is no law against these things!

Galatians 5:22–23 (NLT)

Then he said to me, "Prophesy to these bones and say to them, 'Dry bones, hear the word of the Lord! This is what the Sovereign Lord says to these bones: I will make breath enter you, and you will come to life. I will attach tendons to you and make flesh come upon you and cover you with skin; I will put breath in you, and you will come to life. Then you will know that I am the Lord.

Ezekiel 37:4–6 (NIV)

The Lord said to me, "You have seen correctly, for I am watching to see that my word is fulfilled."

Jeremiah 1:12 (NIV)

Marriage Prayer:

Heavenly Father, I humbly and boldly come before Your throne and ask that Your Spirit comes like a mighty rushing wind to not only prepare my future husband and me, fill us, and move within us, but to bring us together. Lord, give me verses, visions, and wisdom as I pray for our marriage. Show me how to do this and guide me. Also, protect me. I am trusting You, Lord, with my heart, emotions, the relationship, and process. Bring heaven down to earth and unite us—a kingdom marriage and family for Your purposes, our destinies, and all for Your glory. Grow us in You and place a ring of fire around us until You bring us together.

I rebuke all schemes of the enemy and declare him defeated in Jesus' name. No one and nothing can thwart

Your plans, Jesus. I praise You in advance for turning my heart toward my husband and the new You are birthing in both of our souls. I praise You for all You are doing in our lives and for what is to come. Lord, I thank You for choosing him for me and saving him for me. I pray Your anointing and power will be continually on our lives, callings, marriages, families, and all that we say and do. Carry us through this time. May the Holy Spirit be loud and clear, and Your presence be thick, so we can hear and see Your divine guidance. May my prayers and the verses You highlight create a strong foundation for all that is to come, bring us closer to You, and sanctify us through and through so that we can be used entirely for You together as one. Flood us with Your love, grace, mercy, and compassion so that we can have the same holy love for one another. This marriage is for You. Lord, thank you for Your divine guidance, revelations, and constant presence as we move forward. I praise You for going above and beyond all we could ask, think, or imagine. Nothing is impossible with You, and nothing is too hard for You. Your will *will* be done! Show us your glory, Lord! In Jesus' mighty and matchless name, I love you, Amen!

CHAPTER 11

Have You Ever... Sensed Seasons Were Changing?

Your own ears will hear him. Right behind you a voice will say, "This is the way you should go," whether to the right or to the left.

—Isaiah 30:21 (NLT)

Just as lightbulbs burn out, so do certain seasons. I have this old lamp that I love, and it stopped working abruptly. (I find items I love and am determined to keep them for life. I am sentimental like that, I suppose.) I gathered this old lamp probably needed a new lightbulb. The Lord only knows the last time I replaced it. I tried multiple lightbulbs. Nothing. Sigh, it must be broken, so much to my dismay, off to the store, I went to purchase a new one. The new lamp required a three-way bulb, and upon returning home, I thought, why not try this bulb in my old lamp, as well? Ta-da! It was not broken at all. It just needed the right bulb. Thankfully, my favorite light worked again, and my blonde moment was remedied. A brand new lamp was necessary to gain that revelation. Oh, that we wouldn't be so quick to believe you cannot save some situations! Sometimes it only takes a small change to unveil a solution for revival. Unfortunately, though, this season didn't have a quick fix, nor could it be restored (at least right now).

Have you ever had a season like that? The end was drawing near, signaling you to prepare, yet you couldn't fully comprehend the scope of the scenario upon you or how the details would shake out on the other side. You may have felt the circumstances were undone, and moving on was necessary without the satisfaction of completion. I can relate. This ending felt messy and wide open for either an eternal question mark to reside at the end or an opportunity for another storyline to be penned. In many aspects, this chapter in the unexpected narrative God was writing hadn't gone how I anticipated in the least bit. (Does it ever?)

As the season dimmed, I saw a vision of the Lord beckoning me forward. He wasn't upset or in a hurry. He waved His arm gently, motioning me onward as if saying, "*I need you over here. Come on. It is okay. Get behind me.*" A new lane. A new rhythm. Leaving something undone and on God's autopilot to shift, refocus, and move forward. It was a strange sensation, yet His call settled undoubtedly throughout my bones. It was time.

The New Year burst forth with hope and anticipation. However, there was this prompting in my spirit that everything was about to change. The season was ending, and things would be entirely transformed in multiple areas of my life. God had impressed it upon my heart that if I genuinely desired the life I had prayed for (and He promised), I needed to learn how to build a life and not just work or build a business. Some adjustments needed to be made. (Sounds fun, huh?)

My parents came to visit for spring break that year, and while they were here, we saw the following verse three different times in the most unusual places. Philippians 4:13 (NKJV): "I can do all things through Christ who strengthens me." Whenever God repeats Himself, especially in sets of threes, I pay attention. I wrote that verse down in my journal, but in total transparency due to the enduring required from the former years, I tucked it away in the farthest corner of my mind. I focused on the more pleasant words God had promised for that year because I couldn't handle thinking difficulty was ahead. It was too overwhelming. I was grateful for the warning (I don't want Him to stop doing that! I need all the heads up I can get!), but I didn't want the verse to be twisted by the enemy and perpetuate worry.

No matter how much I pushed the heaven-sent signal to the background, it remained—blinking incessantly. Patiently pursuing my attention and reminding me not to fear but realize massive upheaval was knocking at my door.

Shortly after my parents left, Freya and I huddled up in my prayer closet to chat with God. With my elbows propped up on my knees and my hands opened with childlike faith, I asked God to remove from my hands what was no longer necessary for this upcoming season and to place in them what was. I continued by asking God for wisdom and guidance on multiplying what He was bringing. I wanted to be a good steward of the gifts and walk in abundance as I let go of what had become familiar in my promise-land. God heard me, and His answer came like lightning. I arrived the following day at the organization that God had so miraculously sent me into and was met with the news that my position was no longer available in the context I was currently working. All I could think was, "That was fast! Okay, Lord, here we go."

Since that door was closing and the stream of income would be lost, I began asking God, "What should I replace it with?" I sat up quickly in my bed two days later with this wild idea to start an exclusive by referral only pet sitting business. My first response was, "You want me to pet sit!?" I didn't see that coming, but I was excited! That is how Premier Pet Sitting was born, which would become one of the most healing and liberating opportunities God could have created in this tough time of transition. It also gave me ample opportunities to secretly pray for folks and their homes as God sent me into new territory (another covert Alicia op)! That alone thrilled me! I was like, "Sign me up, Lord!" (I am sure you have caught on by now that my heart is bent enthusiastically toward adventure! I don't do dull very well. I concur with Helen Keller—life is either a daring adventure or nothing at all. I could use a few boring days, though, after these past six years, but only a few.)

Pet sitting may have seemed like a strange direction to go and a small door of opportunity, but may I encourage you? Those small doors God opens often lead to bigger ones. Choose to walk through even if it seems small, counterintuitive, and unlikely. I was thankful for this new strategy and relieved because this seemed like the perfect plan to slide into obscurity for a bit. Plus, who doesn't love spending time with cute pups and other furry friends? It is all smiles, an abundance of treats, and the silent moments of implied understanding are unparalleled.

Following that unexpected plot twist, the surrealist day of my latter years arrived with little warning. One loss was already under my belt, but this next one was startling. The business in the health and fitness industry that I had been building for six years was reorganized, which equated to a substantial loss in income with little security regarding a paycheck in the coming days. I will likely not forget the day that announcement shattered my norm and carefully laid plans. That was a difficult day. The kind of day that stops your whole world, and time passes without much recollection of the minutes or hours, and you cannot remember if you ate. (You know it's a big deal because eating is not something I forget to do!) Ever had a day like that? They are unsettling and life-altering.

The following morning, while trying to process and figure out what this newfound announcement meant for my business and future, I walked through my kitchen, and peace flowed over me. From the top of my head to the tip of my toes, I was oddly calm. Then came relief, which instantly caused pangs of guilt because how could I be relieved when so many, including myself, were facing this tremendous loss? Even so, a substantial weight lifted off my shoulders. I hadn't realized how much I was carrying, and for the first time, I felt freer. I said, "God, that has to be You because that is not how I should feel right now." From a surrendered evening in my prayer closet to watching the pieces of my life crumble around me, the most remarkable transition yet had begun...

Verses to Declare:

I hear the Lord saying, "I will stay close to you, instructing and guiding you along the pathway for your life. I will advise you along the way and lead you forth with my eyes as your guide. So don't make it difficult; don't be stubborn when I take you where you've not been before. Don't make me tug you and pull you along. Just come with me!

Psalm 32:8–9 (TPT)

See, I am doing a new thing! Now it springs up; do you not perceive it? I am making a way in the wilderness and streams in the wasteland.

Isaiah 43:19 (NIV)

No one's ever seen or heard anything like this, never so much as imagined anything quite like it—What God has arranged for those who love him. But you've seen and heard it because God by his Spirit has brought it all out into the open before you.

1 Corinthians 2:9 (MSG)

But if he (thief) is caught, he must pay back seven times what he stole...

Proverbs 6:31 (NLT)

Prayer:

Lord Jesus, thank You for how You warn us of endings, beginnings, and changes. You give the ability to discern the times and seasons, and for that, I praise you! Please continue to pour out that anointing upon me, so I move in step with Your rhythm and occupy the lane You have prepared.

Lord, as seasons change, remove from my hands what is no longer necessary and replace it with Your best—best opportunities, plans, and resources for this next season. I know things are not as they seem. Something bigger is happening in this shaking, and I need Your miracle-working power and saving strength to navigate this whirlwind of circumstances. Help me to see this through Your eyes, Lord. You are my guide, and I declare, wherever You lead, I am going! I am tuning out all distractions and the noise to follow You and You alone. Lord, please teach me Your ways and show me how to work the gifts and opportunities You are entrusting to me.

Nothing is lost when it is in You, Lord, and I am confident You will restore all that belongs to me. I declare that whatever the thief has stolen will be returned to my house seven-fold! The latter part of my life will be greater than the former! Hallelujah! I stand in firm faith as I wait for the unfolding of Your great plans. Thank you, God, for the new and my "next!" In Jesus' name, Amen!

CHAPTER 12

Have You Ever... Experienced a Transition?

You have led me through the fire, and all of my life You have been faithful. Oh I will sing of the goodness of God.

—Bethel Music

Shaking in our lives often accompanies transition. Whether subtle or flagrant, the process may be all together awful and awesome. Those summer months that followed my shaking were a blur. Have you ever experienced such a trying time in your life where everything has crashed, nothing was the same, and you look in the mirror wondering who you are? Right there with you. I felt bereft of any direction, and even if I had an idea, I wasn't sure how to execute it. Here I was again wondering how God would provide and bring me through to the other side. There is nothing quite like seeing the foundational aspects of your life disappear, some you anticipated and others that hit you like a bus. I sat many nights at my kitchen counter sobbing (the ugly cry) and saying two words because that was all I could muster: "Jesus, help!"

As I was feeling like a failure, He spoke with a deep understanding and compassion, *"Oh my precious child, I know. You didn't do anything wrong. There is nothing to be sad about. I have more ahead. Let go and take My Hand. I'll carry you."* And He did—every single day in beautiful and various ways. The verse "Give us this day our daily bread" (Matthew 6:11, NKJV) took on a whole new meaning. I had been living in that mode for many years, but God dialed up the intensity and relevance of that verse during this time. Every day I had the privilege of waking up and asking Him what He wanted me to do and then receiving whatever provision He had. Trust. Faith. I thought the former years required both, but I needed them supercharged for these days.

I know how it feels to lose those significant pieces of day-to-day life that rattle the entire structure. I have experienced the sadness of watching what God seemed to be growing fall apart. I understand the stress of wondering where provision will come from and where God is taking you next. I also know the strength required to keep going during the unknown and unexpected. However, difficult and sad, I have watched God give birth to and accomplish the most beautiful things in the midst of the pain, pressure, and dismantling. We tend to despise challenging times and lack, but I have seen lack initiate more in my life than ease has.

I don't believe every loss during this transition was because God took from me. The enemy had his hand in the mix, stealing and trying to destroy. Although the enemy's schemes may have been in play, God does appoint these seasons of transition and adversity to pull out of us what is necessary for where He is eager to take us. You are made in the image of God, and He has put His greatness inside of you! The dismantling of familiar quite often brings forth that greatness, the makings of your destiny (or at least in my experience, that has been true more often than not), and a more deep-seated reliance on the Lord. These seasons also draw a distinct line between what God can do and what we thought was our own ability. You find out, if you didn't already know, where true blessings and success comes from—only from the Lord. Is it fun? Hardly. Do you sob and feel like you can't withstand it? Some days. Do you get to see God show up and show out? You better believe it!

If God can deliver this small item that my heart cared about, He can provide the big-ticket items! Before this shaking in my life, I had been researching rugs for my living room. I had picked out a few but wasn't interested in spending the money, so I tabled the dream of a fluffy carpeted square that would add an element of home to my apartment. Shortly after, I heard a knock on my apartment door. My neighbor was moving, and she said, "I have this rug I never used. Would you like it?" It was almost exactly like the ones I had been staring at online earlier: same color and similar design. God brought me a rug! There is nothing He cannot do! It wasn't something I needed, but He knew I wanted it. He also knew that this was part of me learning how to make a home and build a life. I stood in my living room crying and laughing while saying out loud, "God, you brought me a rug!" (Like He didn't know.) That rug adorned my living room floor as a reminder of His faithfulness and goodness.

You will never convince me God doesn't care. He cares more than we can fathom, and if you need something today, I am convinced He is working on bringing it to you! It may come through an unlikely door, but don't hesitate to open it! If you are in that painful place of shaking and transition, please go ahead and mourn. Lay at His feet. Cry ugly tears. Lament. He can handle the emotions and cries of your heart, and if you can only muster these two words like I did, "Jesus! Help," then that is sufficient. He is running to you, friend. He is running, and He won't tarry one minute.

It is in these tumultuous times that we press in even more to Him. I remember someone asking me, "Aren't you doing this and that?" (Insert all the well-meaning advice you have ever been given.) My answer was no because, in my heart, the only place I needed to be was in the presence of the Father. He was the only One who could make a way and direct my steps. I only wanted His plan. I prayed for the income He had with my name on it. That is the blessed and favored kind! No matter how great it looks, not every opportunity has our names on it, so be careful what you say yes to, especially in times of uncertainty. Remember, Child of God, you are not desperate. You want the opportunities ordained by heaven because there won't be strings attached! There was a barrage of people who criticized and attempted to bully me in various directions. Some were trying to help, and others were pushing for their agenda. Not everyone is for you or will understand the paths we walk and what God calls us to. We smile and give grace but turn our face to the One who is, does, and always will.

Are you sitting in a place where there looks to be no way out? Are you in a season of unexpected change and maybe despair? God is there, collecting your tears and smoothing out the path ahead. He has provision coming and the answer to whatever your pressing need may be. He will lift you above the distress and anguish your heart is feeling to carry you. He has doors opening that no man can shut (Revelation 3:8, KJV), and your gift(s) will make room for you (Proverbs 18:16, NKJV). It will bring a fulfillment that you couldn't concoct from your best-laid plans.

I am not privy to what your current or previous transitions have looked like, but I guess you felt that same wide range of emotions I did. (Quite possibly all within the same hour. Can I get an amen?) Transition is hard. It is painful. Rarely simple. It is stripping. It is refreshing. It is miraculous. It is purifying. It is nerve-racking, but God always makes the transition worth the trip!

Juggling every facet of this seemed more than I could handle, but then God upped the ante! I started working on a local church project for a new small group within their sports life ministry. It began as a simple concept: a group of believers getting together to pray and learn to walk in grace yet truth regarding our nutrition and fitness, but God had bigger ideas. After much discussion about what this group would entail and trying to follow God's lead, the pastor said, "It would be great if there were an outline for the group of what each week's lesson would be." After a long pause, I said, "So you want me to write a study?" His response was, "Yes."

I thought this couldn't have come at a worse time. I had almost zero income, my emotions were a wreck, and what each day would bring was a mystery, but it was clear there was no advancing until I wrote a curriculum and study. I sat on that for a minute. I was glad and curious regarding what God was up to with this newfound assignment, but I was also slightly exasperated that He would add this to my plate. It was a divine moment, a setup, and God was using this pressure and rearrangement to help me. (Repeat after me—God is trying to help me. It may not feel like it, but that is true for your transition too!)

The last two weeks of July, I cleared my entire schedule (there wasn't much on my calendar anyway) and escaped from reality to write. I hiked. I wrote. I wept. I lay on the grass. I watched the ducks. I wrote some more. I wore a hat daily. (Sometimes, you need more than dry shampoo to cover up reality!) I took a selfie in the middle of the river once, and it was from a far away angle because no one needed to see my eyes. Can we say Puffy McPufferson? There wasn't enough eyeliner or mascara in all of Ulta to veil the dismal condition that my eyes were reflecting. It was a far stretch from glamorous. I am not sure writing or creating ever is, especially when it comes from a place of personal experience. I wrote under a bridge in my favorite spot on the river most days. Hidden and dealing with my pain and thoughts while words spilled out upon the pages of my notebook. I was in disarray, but God was not, and I began to see the beauty He was crafting upon those pages. My agony and journey would become someone else's blessing, which was the most awe-inspiring and rejuvenating thought. I remember telling God, "Are you sure? I think I should be working, not writing," but in my heart, I felt Him say, "*This is the work I have for you right now.*"

Has God ever asked you to do something that seemed like the complete opposite of what was needed? That is when we trust Him greater than ever because He doesn't set us up to fail. Quite the contrary, He is setting us up to succeed beyond our imagination if we let Him.

It was late fall when the final copy of the curriculum and study was approved and sent to print. I walked to my car that day and thought, "You just birthed a ministry, Lord!" I was overwhelmed by His goodness and mercy. I didn't have the wherewithal to turn the ignition in my car. I sat in the parking lot for a good while, soaking that moment in. It was surreal and made me bawl to think God had done this through one of the roughest and most unstable times of my life.

A few chapters back, I mentioned the story about how God asked me to lay down my dreams during the prayer assignment that He had given me years ago. Well, this was one of them—a ministry. Being in and having a ministry has been spoken over my life in various ways throughout the past decade. My businesses had been built upon the premise of ministry years ago when I prayed, "God take this business and make it ministry. It has to be bigger than me." This new facet was an expansion. One I had dreamed of, yet with no comprehension of how it would come to pass. There I sat in the parking lot of a church that I didn't know existed when I moved to Texas, and God brought it to fruition through the kindest and most honoring culture I had the privilege of being a part of.

God sent the most incredible people to assist me in the birthing of this ministry. I have heard many times that God has people for you and will help you with your destiny. They will truly see you as God does and the gifts He has placed inside of you. I saw that so clearly during this experience. I have no doubt God turned that pastor's heart toward this project to envision something I couldn't. He walked with me a full year to bring this study to completion and kick off the community group. He was under no obligation to do that. He also didn't have to lend his Biblical expertise, but he readily did. He provided the missing piece of the puzzle because although what was written was right, I felt something was missing—something more profound, more concrete with additional Biblical substance. (What I like to call "meat!" You know, like Wendy's says, where's the beef?) That missing piece of the puzzle was the commentary aspect, and since seminary isn't a part of my background, it didn't occur to me to utilize a commentary.

Thank God for those people He sends with gifts to add to our own. Aren't you glad for the Body of Christ? I sure am. Together we are capable of so much more than when alone. And that, my friends, is how the *A Strong and Healthy Life* curriculum and Bible study were born. God birthed something new in my life to complement what I had experienced and enjoyed! A new beginning was here. It was humbling, healing, scary, redemptive, and a breath of fresh air to my parched and vulnerable soul.

None of this would have happened either had I not lost my previous structure and income because there was no room for me to take on any more responsibility. God knew I wouldn't be able to leave certain situations or people on my own. (I am no quitter.) He allowed the losses to set me free for what He wanted to do in the "next." There was a new position that God needed me to take. It is hard to imagine, but there is protection built into these moments too. God may be protecting you from being where you are no longer meant to be because it wouldn't serve you well or help the situation. He knows what is best, and if you are in a similar place of change, He is just making some room in your life too!

Most would say I lost everything, but even in that excruciating rearrangement, deep down, I was convinced I had gained everything. I watched Him prosper my health and fitness business under the new compensation plan in amounts I had not earned under the old one. I watched Him bring clients for pet sitting that I would have never met otherwise and who paid more than I had invoiced. I watched Him comfort me in moments of deep distress, turn my mourning into dancing, and birth new opportunities and dreams. Supernatural joy flooded my life. I watched Him expand and open my heart for aspects of life that had been muted over the years. I felt Him restoring, making all things new, and providing hope where there was none. He carried me when I couldn't hold myself together (which was often). I watched Him sustain my bank account when there was no income. The complete upheaval brought me closer to my family, and I certainly wouldn't have made it without their support. Lastly, He healed me from the inside out. As each day passed, I was freer and slowly being restored but at the same time, coming into a newly fashioned by the Hand of the Potter Himself version of me.

As you already know, I have a pet sitting business, and it was a source of great healing during my transition. At that time, I met a sweet girl with two of the most adorable golden retrievers. After watching her dogs for a week, we exchanged our goodbyes, but then God stepped in. We began to chat about church and seeing each other there when she asked me about the class I taught on Wednesday nights. I explained to her the premise of *A Strong and Healthy Life*, and her response was, "I should hire you to teach my staff!" And she did. I never imagined God could put that together—from writing a study by the river to pet sitting to teaching my course at a non-profit, but He did, and He already knew what would transpire before I set foot into her home. If He can do that, what can our God not do?

Is God taking you through a transition where you thought everything was lost, yet you can see Him building and rearranging the pieces into something new? You have gained more than what seems lost, too, even if you cannot see the evidence yet. He never removes anything from our lives without bringing better. He plans to prosper you even in the toughest times (Jeremiah 29:11, NIV). I promise that the unfolding of His plan gets more beautiful as you see Him ever so tenderly craft together the broken and missing pieces. He is masterful at creating something out of nothing and tailoring making the outcome. You will nestle into that new space with a sense of belonging and being home. You will fit perfectly. Wait until you see Him use the gifts, blessings, and opportunities He births! You will jump with joy at the goodness flowing from the rearrangement—not just in your own life but how the experience multiplies through others' lives every time you share and walk in the new! The latter has brought me to my knees in awe of God more than once! He uses everything for our good, but when it blesses someone else and goes forth to bear fruit in their lives, it's restitution bursting forth with celebration! Joy multiplied. Healing multiplied. Freedom multiplied. Blessings multiplied. God's glory multiplied! There are exponential increases and expansion in every direction! That is the kingdom of God (to which you belong)!

As God rearranges, don't be afraid to wait on Him. There may be pressure from every side, but tune your ears toward heaven so you move in the right direction. Be obedient and do whatever He puts on your plate regardless of how the situation looks and no matter how challenging the task may seem. He is setting you up and repositioning you. He is the God of breakthrough and is taking you to an expected end! He will get it right. Embrace the transition. Promotion is on the other side, and it's next level, friend! Get ready. Get ready. Get ready!

Verses to Declare:

You've kept track of all my wandering and my weeping. You've stored my many tears in your bottle—not one will be lost. For they are all recorded in your book of remembrance.

Psalm 56:8 (TPT)

"Each time he said, 'My grace is all you need. My power works best in weakness.' So now I am glad to boast about my weaknesses, so that the power of Christ can work through me. That's why I take pleasure in my weak-

nesses, and in the insults, hardships, perse-
cutions, and troubles that I suffer for Christ.
For when I am weak, then I am strong.

2 Corinthians 12:9–10 (NLT)

This is what the Lord says: "Stop at the cross-
roads and look around. Ask for the old, godly
way, and walk in it. Travel its path, and you
will find rest for your souls."

Jeremiah 6:16 (NLT)

A new song for a new day rises up in me every time I think about how he breaks through
for me! Ecstatic praise pours out of my mouth
until everyone hears how God has set me free.
Many will see his miracles; they'll stand in
awe of God and fall in love with him!

Psalm 40:3 (TPT)

Instead of your shame you will receive a double portion, and instead of disgrace you will
rejoice in your inheritance. And so you will
inherit a double portion in your land, and everlasting joy will be yours.

Isaiah 61:7 (NIV)

When God made his promise to Abraham, he backed it to the hilt, putting his own reputation on the line. He said, "I promise that I'll bless you with everything I have—bless and bless and bless!" Abraham stuck it out and got everything that had been promised to him. When people make promises, they guarantee them by appeal to some authority above them so that if there is any question that they'll make good on the promise, the authority will back them up. When God wanted to guarantee his promises, he gave his word, a rock-solid guarantee—God can't break his word. And because His word cannot change, the promise is likewise unchangeable.

Hebrews 6:14–18 (MSG)

Prayer:

Dear God, help! I know Your grace is sufficient for me in all things and at all times, but this is hard. Please carry me, Lord. Thank you for being my ever-present help in time of need and this transition. I surrender and place my feelings of distress and agony in Your hands. When I am weak, Lord, You make me strong! Please give me faith every morning to rely solely on You and be okay with that. I don't have to figure this out because

You already have! I may be weeping now, but joy will come in the morning! Thank you, Lord!

Even though this is painful, I long to become and behold what You have ordained. Please continue to mold, transform, and make room in my life so I can inherit the next level and plans You have for me. Lord, may each tear I have shed water seeds that will blossom into a beautiful garden, rich in faith. I believe You will honor my faith and bring a great and plentiful harvest! Lord, please keep my feet moving in the direction of the old, godly way. Infuse me with the courage to walk through the doors assigned to me and acquire the provision that You have set aside. May I be wise with my "yeses" in this season and guard my heart and mind. Thank you, Lord, for my inheritance, the perfect plans You have for my life, and all You are birthing in my transition. I declare and decree a double portion, exponential increase, and expansion are coming, and I receive it! Your promises are a sure thing!

Please bring those people to assist me with my dreams and add to my gifts so we can do more incredible things for You! May I have an open heart to receive those You have chosen to walk with me to destiny and whatever I put my hands to prosper for Your Name's sake. I am rejoicing Lord today not only for the promotion and the birthing but the lives that will be touched and forever changed because of this journey. May those who experience the fruit from this transition be blessed, recognize the miracles, and fall in love with You! Be big, God, be big! I am choosing to sing a new song today, and I believe You are breaking through for me! In Jesus' name, Amen!

Yadah

(Hebrew)—to shoot arrows, praise, and give
thanks. Worship became my new weapon and
prophetic declaration.

CHAPTER 13

Have You Ever... Needed Rest?

You rest. I will do it. ~ God

What is your reaction when you hear God say, "rest?" How does that make you feel? Out of control? Relieved? Grateful? Lost? Ready to shout Hallelujah? I felt those emotions, and it was strange and wonderful. No striving. No pressure. No plan. Nothing but sweet rest and waiting on the Lord to bring provision, show me the path to take every day, and set the pace. A new rhythm—one in step with heaven drenched with purpose and sparkling with holy anticipation. I was at rest for the first time in years. It was a bone-deep rest that blanketed my entire being. Some days I wondered if I was alive because this type of rest was so out of character for me! I felt no need to speak or share what was happening.

God hid me. He sheltered me. I may have been scared, but I had never been freer. Free from all titles and labels. Free from the pressure of trying to be and do more. Free from building a platform and promotion. Free from the grind. It is beautiful when God helps us shed what is weighing us down. I loved my life before, but I wasn't at rest, nor was I was always present. I was continually striving and building, and that wasn't a life well-lived.

During this season of mandated rest and solitude in Him, God brought me to Elijah's story in 1 Kings 17:1–16 (NIV). As I summarize this story (Read it for yourself though! God has something for you tucked away in the details!), I believe you will be able to see from previous chapters how much truth flows from it. The Lord directed Elijah to go and hide. He was fed by ravens while isolated, the familiar brook dried up, and God told him where to go next. Not to mention the miracle with the widow! A note of encouragement if you are in a similar season—there will be miracles!

I was comforted by Elijah's story and felt God speaking. I desperately needed to hear Him and be encouraged that He was indeed at the helm of the story being written. Was it easy? Of course not. But even in isolation, I didn't want to go back to living under the labels and constraints that I had before. It wasn't that the prior structure was bad or necessarily wrong. It was what the previous season required and was supposed to be. However, when God does a new thing, He does a new thing, and the old habits and structures won't fit. We tend to want God to do new things and give us a fresh start, yet expect to be able to hang on to the old or control and fit the recent move of God into this neat little familiar box. I have bad news, but I am sure you have already had this realization. That is not how the fairytale goes.

There may be patterns and familiar processes. (I can see this in my own story! I often think, "I have been here before," even if the circumstances are slightly different. Can you say the same?) However, there will also be an element of surprise and mystery with God because He wants us to rely on Him and not some formula or method. If we live with the notion that we control God or expect Him to move only in ways we are familiar with, then we are not honoring Him as God, are we? Your previous experiences with His faithfulness and miracles build trust. We should hold onto those as reminders (the Bible refers to these as Stones of Remembrance in Joshua 4), but that doesn't necessarily mean He will answer again in the same fashion. In the new, we have to trust His nature and character and the fact that He is God. Let's not let our lack of faith or trust limit Him, amen? Our God has no limits.

Rest is beautiful and challenging. It requires much faith and willingness to sit and wait. It challenges us to yield, seek the Lord, dig deeper, explore ways to grow, and bring forth what He is trying to birth in us. Those pauses have a purpose. It will feel awkward, but in those pauses, we find our truer selves, our significance in the Lord, and what matters most. We learn to relinquish control, allowing God to fight and provide for us, and we have a fresh encounter with Him that invokes a new depth of intimacy. We must open our hearts, let go, and stand in the in-between long enough to receive what He is bringing.

I am an introvert by nature, but this abrupt slow-down and the newly discovered fact that no one need-ed me was challenging. That was a significant change! Helping others and being needed gave me great sat-isfaction, but this slowdown revealed gaps in my own life where I forgot to set boundaries. (Does anyone else struggle with that? Boundaries are a whole rant in itself, right?) God was not only allowing patterns and habits to surface that I hadn't addressed, but He was giving me ample time to listen as He poured out visions, dreams, and prophecy. It was during this time that God pulled me deeper into these areas of my spiritual walk. I had time to ponder, dig in the Bible, and research. It was astonishing how He would lead and reveal. I loved every minute of immersing myself and absorbing the fresh revelations. He kept calling me deeper. His gentle voice gave reassurance, *"Stay in the secret place. Hidden in the darkness, protected, and covered. There is room here to grow and transform."*

As that guidance poured forth, I had this vision of a giant shield. I was underneath, and there was room to move around, yet I was hidden and protected. I felt like this miniature version of myself under such a massive and weighty shield. It was then that I realized this was also a time of consecration. Transition and transformation often require that. He will draw you into the secret place with Him to set you apart. God was also giving me a new operating system—new revelations, directions, and mindset for this season and beyond. In the new, you won't be able to react or move in the same way. It will require a different version of you! If you are isolated in your rest and transformation, I promise that, as we like to say in the Midwest, "He has not hung you out to dry." You are safe. You are protected. He is highly involved in the process.

The world stood still for me. I sat for hours and enjoyed His company and indulged myself in every morsel He poured out. It reminded me of the verse, "We (people) do not live by bread alone but by every word that comes from the mouth of God" (Matthew 4:4, NLT). Read it in The Passion Translation, "Bread alone will not satisfy, but true life is in every word, which constantly goes forth from God's mouth."

Oh, how I love that! He is continually speaking and what He gives sustains us supernaturally. It is sweet. It fills you! What are you praying for God to do in your "pause?" Are you seeking Him even though there is likely this insatiable push to stay busy and cram your days full of distractions or try to fix it on your own? Rest in Him. Come away with Him and savor the time of silence and slowness. He has extraordinary and unique gifts, wisdom, and knowledge He wants to share with you. Lean in, friend! God has got some pouring He would like to do!

He birthed many beautiful things out of this period of rest but what I love most is who He transformed me to be. I am more myself—the purest version—yet forever changed. It was like being stuck in a dark cocoon for months, trying to figure out who I was and who I was becoming. I had several dreams of caterpillars before and during this period which couldn't have been more on point! One of my favorites involved a dead caterpillar on my hand. It was stuck to me like it had been burnt into my skin. There was this gentleman in the dream (symbolic of Jesus) who tenderly took my hand, examined the bug with great attentiveness, and carefully peeled it off one tiny section at a time. Almost as if it had created a deep scar that needed tending to. I replied in my dream, "Thank you for helping me even though that hurt." Transformation and healing go hand in hand. Be patient as you rest and let Jesus tend to your wounds. He wants to take your pain away. You can trust Him with your scars. He is gentle even though He is intentional.

Even spiritually, I could not use the same methods as I had in the past to battle or overcome. I couldn't intercede as I previously had. I was muzzled in my speech like silence was only appropriate. I had difficultly writing and formulating my thoughts. Ideas, revelations, insights, and cries of my heart swirled around inside of me with no outlet. I couldn't wage war in prayer like I had before. I couldn't listen to the same sermons or content or even read books. In this period of transformation and rest, God made a singular practice my focus—worship. I could sing, and I could dance. It didn't appear to be the most suitable time for either, but if God says it, then it must be what is needed and what He wants most from us!

I was learning that declarations with scripture and intercession in the form of prayer weren't the only ways to fight my battles. Worship not only changed my focus and transformed my heart but lifted my eyes toward heaven and allowed me to interact with God in a way that was solely focused on Him and adoration. He was teaching me worship was a mighty weapon, and it became a prophetic act as well as I continued to learn and grow. Here are a few verses that encouraged me during this time, and I pray they do the same for you! Prayer is powerful, but worship, that moves the heart of God differently and ushers in His presence.

A time to cry and a time to laugh. A time to grieve and a time to dance.

Ecclesiastes 3:4 (NLT)

But thou art holy, O thou that inhabitest the praises of Israel.

Psalm 22:3 (KJV)

God's high and holy praises fill their mouths, for their shouted praises are weapons of war!

Psalm 149:6 (TPT)

Now for those of you who know me, you are already aware God didn't bless me with vocals. I love singing and dancing (despite my questionable moves), and I think that is because I am not good at either, yet the Lord doesn't give a hoot and delights in me anyway. I am not obligated to be anything but His daughter in these moments. (Neither are you.) No facade. Completely free. Praising my King. Awkward, out of tune, and unhindered. Just me. And as much as this season of transition, transformation, and rest were a recalibration of epic proportions, it was also so I could be and do just that—be me, learn to live life again, let the unnecessary standards of this world fade away, and love Jesus even more than before. I adored what God had done, and the thought of putting old constraints back on and returning to the previous rhythms made every fiber of being stand up and yell, "No!" It was at that moment I knew God completed a significant work and miracle in making all things new in and around me.

If you can relate to the oscillating extremes of transformation and rest that resemble a very unpredictable seesaw where at a moment's notice, you go from laughter to tears to collapsing in exhaustion and then bursts of nervous energy trying to take back control and force yourself from the solitary, stuck place, I promise you will be okay. More than okay! You are in the Potter's Hands, and that is the safest place to be. Stay hidden under the canopy of His love as He transforms you. Let Him pour out His grace and strategy upon you. He will nurture, provide, and lead you into the promises that have been stamped upon your life by His Hand alone.

Oh, and don't forget to sing your new song and break out some of your dance moves while you are at it! (Perhaps a little undignified dancing like David is in order? For whatever reason, my kitchen seems to be the place random dance parties break out most often!) You have got a lot of reasons to cut loose and worship your little heart out! He is ushering in an outcome and transformation that will radiate a stunning display of the Father's love, kindness, goodness, power, and authority. You are breaking out of the cocoon and preparing to fly—healed, consecrated for the next God-purpose of your life, freer than you ever imagined, and to heights you haven't dreamed of yet! Until then, rest.

> R—*remember all God has done.*
> E—*exchange your way for His and embrace some fun!*
> S—*slow down to strengthen your mind, soul, and frame.*
> T—*trust in the One who never puts you to shame.*

And when my mind couldn't stop pondering the ifs, ands, and buts, God quietly reminded me, *"Trust Me. I have got you."* He has you too, sister, and will satisfy you deeply while you wait.

Verses to Declare:
> He who dwells in the secret place of the Most High shall abide under the shadow of the Almighty.
>
> Psalm 91:1 (NKJV)

> For only we who believe can enter his rest.
>
> Hebrews 4:3 (NLT)

Are you weary, carrying a heavy burden? Come to me. I will refresh your life, for I am your oasis. Simply join your life with mine. Learn my ways, and you'll discover that I'm gentle, humble, easy to please. You will find refreshment and rest in me. For all that I require of you will be pleasant and easy to bear.

Matthew 11:28–30 (TPT)

He says, "Be still, and know that I am God."

Psalm 46:10 (NIV)

But we all, with unveiled face, beholding as in a mirror the glory of the Lord, are being transformed into the same image from glory to glory, just as by the Spirit of the Lord.

2 Corinthians 3:18 (NKJV)

God can provide for his lovers even while they sleep!

Psalm 127:2 (TPT)

Ever since I first heard of your strong faith in the Lord Jesus and your love for God's people everywhere, I have not stopped thanking God for you. I pray for you constantly, asking God, the glorious Father of our Lord Jesus Christ, to give you spiritual wisdom and insight so that you might grow in your knowledge of God. I pray that your hearts will be flooded with light so that you can understand the confident hope he has given to those he called—his holy people who are his rich and glorious inheritance. I also pray that you will understand the incredible greatness of God's power for us who believe him. This is the same mighty power that raised Christ from the dead and seated him in the place of honor at God's right hand in the heavenly realms.

Ephesians 1:15–20 (NLT)

Praise the Lord! Praise God in his sanctuary; praise him in his mighty heaven! Praise him for his mighty works; praise his unequaled greatness! Praise him with a blast of the ram's horn; praise him with lyre and harp! Praise him with tambourine and dancing; praise him with strings and flutes! Praise him with a clash of cymbals; praise him with loud clanging cymbals. Let everything that breathes sing praises to the Lord! Praise the Lord!

Psalm 150:1–6 (NLT)

Prayer:

Lord God, I lay reverently at Your feet. You are worthy of all the praise. Today, I come before You as Your humble servant and precious Daughter to lift my hands and worship You. Holy, holy, holy is the Lord God Almighty! You are the King of glory! You are mighty! You are magnificent! You are everything to me! I worship You for who You are, all that You have done, and for what is to come. I declare I am singing and dancing my way through this! May these acts of worship and shouts of praise usher in Your presence, bring me closer to You, and send shockwaves into the enemy's camp! Let God arise, and His enemies scatter! I rejoice that this is the beginning, not the ending! You fight my battles! I am protected! You are my supplier! You are the one true God, and there is none like You!

Thank you, Lord, for transforming and taking me from glory to glory. Thank you for caring about my inner and physical healing as well as my growth, needs, and desires. Please tend to my scars, Lord, and place Your healing balm upon them. Supernaturally remove anything that may still be festering and causing pain, even if I am unaware of it. Slough off those dead things, Lord! May my life display Your wondrous glory, and may this transformation mark me in such a way that people will see You in and through me. Have Your way, Lord.

I praise You for the provision, protection, and safe place to grow that I have in You. What goes forth from this time in the darkness of the cocoon with You will change everything! I receive it! May this time be an oasis where old yokes are removed, a new mantle and anointing falls for such a time as this, and that I become deeply satisfied by You alone. I pray that I will operate from this position of stillness from this day forward—never to return to the old!

Lord Jesus, please continue to make me holy as You are holy and teach me Your rhythms so that I may live lightly and freely! Release Your wisdom and knowledge and flood me with Your light. I may feel lowly now, but You are raising me up! I declare I am being upgraded, commissioned, and am getting ready to fly! To soar all for the glory of God! In Jesus' precious and holy name, I pray, Amen!

CHAPTER 14

Have You Ever...
Hit Your Limit?

His eye is on the sparrow, and I know He watches over me.
—Charles Gabriel

At this point, you may be thinking, Can this fairytale get any more challenging? I don't know that it did or if the events' intensity were due to a compounding effect, but as the calendar pages fluttered into the late fall like the leaves falling from the trees, I had hit my limit. I have this saying that I use when I am at that point in my emotions, "I have hit my limit. I need a minute." It often rolls off my tongue accompanied with laughter, but it is serious business when I break out that line! (Do you have a phrase that gets the point across even if you are trying not to be too serious about the situation? I would guess you have some good ones!)

Chaos ensued. I am sure you are familiar with this kind. The kind where you shout in exasperation, "I can't even make this kind of stuff up!" To avoid taking you down a rabbit hole and to provide succinctness to this portion of the story, here are some of the finer and slightly dramatic plot lines of October that made me wonder if I was going to make it. I do have to say, though, that whenever it seems like one ridiculous event after the other is hitting your life, whether, in the natural or spiritual, that is sometimes a solid indication the enemy is putting up one last desperate fight, and he is terrified. He knows you are about to win, so hang on tight!

First, I thought I had lost someone's cats. I looked everywhere in their house and concluded they had escaped, and I needed to apologize and refund their money. I was heartbroken and beside myself. Secondly, my car began having random fits of protest and became quite a character in her old age. Millie (That was my car's name. Please tell me you name yours!) was in the shop more often than on the road, which occurred at the most inopportune times. Nothing like trying to walk dogs, get a rental car, personal train clients, and tow your vehicle multiple times in the same week. She also thought it was quite cute to lock and unlock particular doors on a whim (tsk, tsk). Thirdly, my birthday came and went without much fanfare. I treated myself to an expensive dinner because part of the growth God had placed upon my heart was taking time to live and celebrate the precious moments of life. As it turns out, I don't care much for fancy dinners. Good to know for the future, right? I cried. I left. I ended up having my favorite snack in the car. That was about the only consoling part of the birthday experience. (Happy birthday to me!) Wait, there is more...

My dad ended up in the hospital and was pretty sick. Face-timing with him while he lay in a hospital bed hooked up to IVs and machines was more than my heart could take. That very same day, Millie arrived home only to have another part break.

Toward the end of the month, I dealt with fraudulent purchases made through one of my businesses. One day, my earnings were spectacular, but I logged in the next day, only to find that the wages were pretty much back to zero. With the spiritual warfare and dreams skyrocketing again, I fought for the wherewithal to keep my sanity in check. This Daughter of the King felt more like an unraveling damsel in distress who was at her wit's end.

Have you ever had a day, month, or year like that? I cried out to God emphatically for two specific requests, "Don't take my dad! I cannot handle that right now. Don't take my vehicle either, Lord!" I had parted with so much from my previous life. The only two things that remained were my car and Freya, my cat. I couldn't handle any more disruption. I was hanging on for dear life and needed a smidgen of familiarity to press on. I was fragile, and God knew it. When you cry over the smallest happenstances and cannot handle the slightest change in plans, you have hit your limit. I am naturally a strong person. Most things do not bother me, but this month, I had had it!

What did your last "I am not going to make it" or "I have had it" moment look like? How did God rescue and calm you? I am so thankful we have an ever-present God. I wouldn't be able to persevere without Him, and I am sure you concur. I am writing this, so I guess you have already concluded that I survived the great October of 2019. And, to not leave you hanging, I didn't lose anyone's cats. (Praaaaaaise Jesus, and yes, after all that happened that month, I said it just like that!) It turns out this family of felines are the sneakiest covert creatures I have ever had the pleasure of meeting. Also, my dad is healthy and living his best life. (All the praise hands!) Millie and Freya have their own stories to tell, and those sagas continue but only in brevity. The events of my crazy fall simmered down and fell into place as the rollercoaster of transition began to glide over the horizon and fade away. God allowed the final months of the year to be filled with the calmest, most joyful, and peaceful days. That was a welcomed relief.

You will make it. Say it out loud even if you aren't quite there yet because you will. Don't let the enemy taunt you with chaos. It is a distraction even though it may be real. God has put a limit on his shenanigans. They can only go so far. Your Heavenly Father remembers the promises He made to you even when you don't. They are in good hands—His hands! He has sealed them with His covenant. (Remember the rainbow.) God's got sunshine and blue skies just ahead! As I scanned those same skies for hope and the possibility that a new year holds, I exhaled a deep breath that seemed to be held captive in my lungs for months and realized I had made it. I. Had. Made. It. (Whew!) With my crown straightened and crisis averted, I was guardedly hopeful but at peace and praying the chaos and loss were behind me for good. That wouldn't entirely be the case.

Verses to Declare:

And God said, "This is the sign of the covenant I am making between me and you and every living creature with you, a covenant for all generations to come: I have set my rainbow in the clouds, and it will be the sign of the covenant between me and the earth. Whenever I bring clouds over the earth and the rainbow appears in the clouds, I will remember my covenant between me and you and all living creatures of every kind. Never again will the waters become a flood to destroy all life.

Genesis 9:12–15 (NIV)

He gives food to those who fear him; he always remembers his covenant.

Psalm 111:5 (NLT)

When hope's dream seems to drag on and on, the delay can be depressing. But when at last your dream comes true, life's sweetness will satisfy your soul.

Proverbs 13:12 (TPT)

We rise up and stand firm.

Psalm 20:8 (NIV)

I will answer your cry for help every time you pray, and you will find and feel my presence even in your time of pressure and trouble. I will be your glorious hero and give you a feast. You will be satisfied with a full life and with all that I do for you. For you will enjoy the fullness of my salvation!

Psalm 91:15–16 (TPT)

For he will order his angels to protect you wherever you go. They will hold you up with their hands so you won't even hurt your foot on a stone.

Psalm 91:1–12 (NLT)

Lord, how wonderfully you bless the righteous. Your favor wraps around each one and covers them under your canopy of kindness and joy.

Psalm 5:12 (TPT)

His love broke open the way and he brought me into a beautiful broad place. He rescued me—because his delight is in me! He rewarded me for doing what's right and staying pure.

Psalm 18:19–20 (TPT)

Prayer:

Lord Jesus, for those times when I feel like I can barely hang on, please strengthen my frame. Help me, Lord, to stand firm and look to heaven for hope. I believe You have not forgotten me, and Your promises always come to pass. Lord, I pray to witness signs, wonders, and rainbows as confirmation. I declare favor is my portion, and I am walking under the covering of Your grace and protection. Steady me, Lord.

Today, I bind all chaos in Jesus' name. I declare it is finished, and by Your hand, divine order and stability are coming into my life! I am standing in prayer and faith, believing, just like Daniel (10:1–21, NLT), that even if I have not seen the answer, You have already sent it! Any delay or block by the enemy is annulled today in Jesus' name! Your Word says angels stand guard over me and protect me wherever I go! I am not going under but am coming out on top!

You are a deliverer. You are my deliverer! I believe that day of deliverance is right around the corner, and it will be sweet! Lord, still my soul and refresh my heart with Your joy today. I declare You are bringing me into the broad, beautiful place You have prepared for me. Thank you for fighting for me, delighting in me, and wanting the promises of my life to come to pass more than I even do! I am waiting with great expectation and watching for the feast and celebration that will ever be before me! I praise You, Lord, for how You satisfy, bless, and care for me. You, my glorious Hero, are coming in strong for me! I decree and declare my life will be full, and Your peace will reign. Thank you for the promise that I will not be forsaken, and I will see the goodness of the Lord in the land of the living! In Jesus' mighty name, Amen!

Freya

CHAPTER 15

Have You Ever... Lost a Precious Pet?

One night I had a dream where a violent storm had blown through a house my family and I were staying in and shattered the windows. As the storm dwindled, I ran through the house, crying out in panic. Desperately, I searched for my cat, Freya. She wasn't there. My mom patted my hand and said, "It is almost over." As I looked outside, the scenery was lush with a touch of golden sunlight that happens after a dark storm. The soft light bounced off the water droplets that were nestled on the foliage dispersing into an array of colors. It was serene and peaceful. That dream confirmed that although Freya would be leaving soon and God was preparing my heart for her departure and the remaining losses, there would be light and a bountifulness after the storm.

As much as He prepared me for this moment, you are never entirely prepared to lose a pet, are you? I had just arrived back from a quick trip to Indiana to pick up the new vehicle that I purchased. That evening Freya curled up on my stomach to welcome me home, which was out of character. Normally, she is quick to speak her feelings about being left behind and has no issue keeping me awake until the wee hours of the morning doing so. Not this night. She was eerily quiet. I thought that was odd, but I believe she knew what was coming too. As God was preparing me to let go of her, she was also letting go of me. In some ways, we no longer needed each other. Although, I wholeheartedly wanted to keep her.

God knew it was Freya's time. She had been my best friend and walked with me through some of the most incredible and unbearable times. She traveled with me. She loved to fly (and escape her carrier to saunter the aisleway in true catwalk fashion)! She lived in three states. We studied the Bible and ate snacks together. (We love the Word and food!) She never left my side, but now her purpose and role were fulfilled. It was her turn to frolic onward into her future.

I was grateful for the dreams from the Lord, but the day I had to say goodbye to her was gut-wrenching. If you have had to make that dreaded decision, you know the feeling. It rips your heart out, and it is plain awful. The grief sticks with you, and home doesn't feel the same. A piece is missing.

We took our final ride together with the sunroof wide open and worship tunes playing. It was a fitting wrap-up to those years we had adventured on this earth together. I was grateful she got to ride in my new wheels. (My new vehicle is appropriately named Spirit. We have quite a bit of fun with this as a family!) This ride was a christening of sorts where God symbolically sealed my past and opened a new chapter in my future. It was bittersweet yet a gift from the Lord.

As I dropped her off that day, knowing she would come home to me only as ashes, the tears gushed forth like a spigot with no valve. There I sat in my vehicle with a tear-streaked face as one of the most precious pieces of my life slipped through my hands. The ache of her leaving was more than my already tender and fragmented heart could handle. Tears, tears, and more tears until suddenly, I saw it! God placed a huge rainbow in the sky directly over the vet, where she finally received her well-deserved rest. (Well done, girl, well done.) Smiling through those very same tears that stained my face and drenched my attire, a familiar peace flooded my soul. It was alright. My heart was fully aware of it too. Whatever God was doing, Freya was where she needed to be, even if I had to move ahead without her.

The Lord was quickly removing the final pieces that pointed to my past. We often say, "The past is gone," yet when that is literal and not figurative, that phrase takes on a whole new meaning. For reasons beyond what I could not quite grasp, I recognized these final losses had to happen. However, releasing those things we love and cherish is far from easy. Both my car and Freya had been in my life for fourteen years, and although life moves on and change is inevitable, in my mind, I hadn't envisioned a future without either of them. There was not one ounce of my former life that was physically tangible anymore. God had wiped the slate clean and closed the door.

His peace is something I will never get over. It comes at the most peculiar moments and when you often think that you should have none. What a comforting indicator that He is with us. I wouldn't trade His peace for anything, and I pray His peace falls on you today most remarkably and unmistakably. That, even in your grief, you will have His supernatural comfort and strength to smile through tears and trust His plan for you.

As emotional as this turning point in my fairytale was, grateful was one word that rolled through my mind repeatedly. I was thankful for every minute of the fourteen years Freya and I spent adventuring together. I am guessing as you are reading this, quite possibly even in your grief and deep pools of memories, your heart swells with the same gratitude for your pets (or loved ones) that are gone. Our pets are family and hold such a special place in our hearts and lives. They are one-of-a-kind gifts from the Lord to bless us in ways we never knew we needed or was possible. Aren't you glad God gives us that once-in-a-lifetime chance to love them back? Me too, friend. Me, too. Over the rainbow, they may go but never be forgotten.

Verses to Declare:

And the peace of God, which surpasses all understanding, will guard your hearts and your minds in Christ Jesus.

Philippians 4:7 (ESV)

On the day I called, You answered me; You made me bold with strength in my soul.

Psalm 138:3 (NASB)

Every one of your godly lovers receives even more than what they ask for. For you hear what their hearts really long for and you bring them your saving strength.

Psalm 145:19 (TPT)

Then he broke through and transformed all my wailing into a whirling dance of ecstatic praise! He has torn the veil and lifted from me the sad heaviness of mourning. He wrapped me in the glory garments of gladness. How could I be silent when it's time to praise you? Now my heart sings out loud, bursting with joy — a bliss inside that keeps me singing, "I can never thank you enough!

Psalm 30:11–12 (TPT)

Prayer:

Oh, Lord, I come to You today with a broken heart. I am sad, and the grief is much! The losses we endure on this earth tend to shatter our fragile hearts in ways we cannot describe except with tears and groans. But You are a faithful God. You hold my heart in Your hands and understand. You see every tear. You feel every heartache. You care about every loss. Please heal my heart, and I ask for an outpouring of Your comfort and peace. Wrap them around me like a blanket and etch the sweet memories in my heart and mind as a gift yet bear the burden of loss for me. Please lift me above the grief and sadness and make me bold with strength in my soul. May my core feel Your supernatural strength, confidence, and a deep knowing that it will be okay.

Lord, I love you, and I am thankful for every precious memory with the one I lost and the time You gave me to love them. Thank you for the perfect gifts that You shower in my life as I tread upon this fallen planet. I believe that one day it will all be made right. I stand in faith that although this is painful, You are bringing more from this moment than I know to pray for. I declare You will redeem my pain! Somehow. Someway. You will do it! I cannot praise You enough for that! You are my loving and caring Daddy forever. Hold me tightly and help me through. In Jesus' name, Amen.

CHAPTER 16

Have You Ever... Witnessed the Hand of God in Your Life?

Even miracles take a little time.

—The Fairy Godmother, Cinderella

Does time passing make a miracle any less of a miracle? Oh, I implore you to believe that it does not. Some miracles come by process and time, and sometimes God shows up instantly upon the scenes of our lives with a reminder heaven is closer than we thought. Believe, friend, that no matter however long or short the Lord takes, He still does miracles and has some hand-picked just for you.

If you have made it this far, I am proud of you! The journey has been steep and ever-winding but marked by a delight that sparkles with heaven. Some things haven't changed. My fashion sense is still lacking. (If you see me matching or looking the least bit trendy, I can assure you my two favorite fashionistas, my mom and sister-in-law, put their final touches on the ensemble.) My ability to be unrefined and stand in ridiculous faith is still intact. Baseball caps are still an essential item. Blonde moments continue to mark the majority of my days. My fairytale is still unfolding, but most importantly, God is still moving and doing the impossible, which is my favorite!

At the beginning of 2019, the Lord gave me four words: establishment, exponential, expansion, and embrace. From what you have read thus far, I am sure we can agree that those words seem somewhat contradictory to most of what transpired. But true to His word, even in the messiness, that's what He was doing—in both the spiritual and physical. You might be asking, "Alicia, I thought Texas was your promise-land?" That is still true despite how this fairytale has played out. We often have this image of a promise-land with no pits or trials along the way, but that isn't reality, nor does the Bible support that. The Israelites had the wilderness before they entered their promised land, and there were giants in the land when they arrived! (Sound familiar?)

The majority didn't get to cross that threshold because of their lack of faith! Lord, help us, so that is not our story! Even upon entering the promise-land, they still had to cross the Jordan and take Jericho. Joseph had a literal pit, but God was with him and brought him to his promise-land, the palace (which had its own obstacles), to fulfill the plans and dreams He had given Joseph. Hannah's promise-land lacked one of her biggest heart's desires. She was barren, but even with persistent torment from Peninnah, Hannah remained faithful to God. He heard Hannah's cry and answered her prayer (Exodus 12–18, Numbers 13–14, Joshua 1–6, Genesis 37, 39–46, and 1 Samuel 1–2).

Our promise-lands may not be what we expect, but when they are ordained by God, there is an ease. (I didn't say easy!) Ease is different. It is a flow, favor, and the way in which God is working and has arranged circumstances. I used to tell my parents, "I know things look awful by some people's standards, but my life has never been filled with so much good. Everything is rooted in goodness." That is God. His goodness is not one that is predicated upon circumstances. When we are with God and where He wants us to be, His goodness becomes the heartbeat that permeates every part of the story, even the yuck. The destinations we reach in our God-ordained fairytales matter and have significance, but it is also about who He is fashioning us to be and the promises in the land! How about a little more fun and some miracles before the final pages of this fairytale come to a close?

The Miracle of the Ride

We serve a God of details, and when He shows up, it will make you wonder why you worry or overthink in the first place. Throughout intercession for the gentleman mentioned in previous chapters, God gave me many promises, and some seemed silly. Still, I believe each one had a purpose, and sometimes it's so God can remind us how much He is involved. God repeatedly pointed out the passenger seat in this gentleman's vehicle and that I would sit in it. I thought, "God, right now, he likely doesn't remember my name. How could I possibly ride in his vehicle?"

One evening, a year later, he asked me where I parked my car. I said, "Right there," and pointed just a few spots away. He said, "Get in, and I will take you there." I had honestly forgotten the promise of riding in his vehicle and said, "No, that is okay. I am just right there," and pointed again to a spot only a short distance away. But he was adamant, so I obliged.

The funniest part was he drove me about as far as a couple of parking spaces. I laughed the entire way home that night, saying, "God, you put me in that seat!" Don't ever underestimate our God. He has processes of bringing details to life beyond anything we could put together on our own. It was just a few parking spots. But He did it anyway because He has a personal interest in us, and His plans are greater than we can fathom.

The Miracle of Angel Feathers

That crazy summer where my life appeared to be shambles, God sent the most wonderful signs that heaven was near, and I wasn't alone. One of those signs was the presence of angel feathers. At first, I was thought there must be another source of these feathers! I searched high and low (even tearing apart other people's couches!), but there wasn't. White feathers about size of my palm graced the floors of the most unlikely places. It was as if I was being escorted by angels as I entered the newfound territory and walked by faith. It made me smile, and I hope it does you too. You are guarded carefully (Psalm 91:11, Psalm 34:7, Hebrews 1:14, and Exodus 23:20, NIV).

The Miracle of the New Vehicle and a Home for Millie

Let me take you back just a short jog to set the stage. Remember when I said God prepared me for all that would be falling away in my life, and one of those pieces was Millie, my car? As much as I didn't want to see the old girl go, I was driving one day when the Lord said, *"I need you to buy that vehicle."*

My response was, "Lord, you are going to have to say that again!" I was in no financial position to purchase the vehicle He was referencing, but as time passed, the Lord brought it up again through a vision. I was driving, and as the sun peaked over the highlands here in Hill Country, I had this vision of me unloading my curriculum and Bible study supplies from the back of this grey vehicle. I was overcome with emotion and wept. At that moment, I knew God was using this shift of vehicles to set me up for the next season.

Ironically, I had previously researched this vehicle and initially picked a white one. As the Lord would have it, though, my parents found a grey one in Indiana on my mom's birthday. They didn't know about the grey vehicle in my vision, but that is the one God blessed me to have. It arrived in perfect timing during a month that holds such significance for me—February. This particular February marked three years since my promise-land fairytale began to unfold. (Three in the Bible can mean fullness, completeness, and perfect witness and testimony. Interesting, isn't it?) I can also attest that the vehicle payment had the exact numbers God had been using to speak to me throughout the year. He confirmed that vehicle down to the color and payment!

Millie left shortly after that, and even that is a God story. I hope this tickles you pink because I had to chuckle even in my sadness of seeing her go. God found Millie the perfect home—a sweet lady who understood my emotional attachment to my vehicle and came from

ALICIA KNECHT

a family that loves cars. She even owned a truck named Gary. An old familiar tune blared on the radio as I drove Millie one last time to the front of my apartment complex. The message was clear—peace, be still. That fateful day when I waved goodbye to Millie as she drove off into the sunset, embarking on her next fairytale adventure, pulled at my heartstrings. Perhaps, Millie was getting her happily ever after too. (Don't tell me you aren't even the least bit tickled by that! Mille + Gary!)

I realize you may be reading this and thinking it is just a vehicle. I get that, but the longer you watch God work, the more you realize there is no such thing as "just" anything with Him. He has a hand in all of it and is writing a story with every encounter and detail. To step into the new, we must step out of the old. It no longer fits. Sometimes that even applies to vehicles.

The Miracle in My Finances

About the same time, God was also rearranging my finances. It looked nearly impossible, but earlier that year, He promised my debt would be paid in full. That brought tears to my eyes because it felt as if He was honoring the hard choices I had to make over the past six years. As grateful and faith-filled as I was, I could barely fathom it. A statement I heard multiple times throughout the year from Him was, *Check your mailbox.* I kept thinking, *Who on earth is going to mail that kind of money!*

True to His word, the special delivery did show up in my mailbox, and the senders had no idea they had fulfilled a promise by sending the blessing via snail mail.

I haven't ever cried as many tears of humility or joy. This gift gave me a newfound appreciation for the meaning of the Cross and Jesus paying our debt in full, entirely blameless, and not His to repay. His sacrifice is nothing we deserve, but out of love, He willingly took on our debt of sin and did so with JOY (Hebrews 12:2, NIV). I couldn't help but see the parallels and same love through my own debt story. It will stay with me for the rest of my days.

The Miracle of Long-Awaited Answers to Prayers

As I was writing this book, I pulled out my old prayer and vision sheet that I had brought to Texas. It was the one that shortly after arriving, God said, was complete. I didn't hold any of the answers to those prayers in my hands, but I obediently wrote *"It is finished"* across the middle of the page and tucked it away, anxiously awaiting God to pour out a fresh vision. As I recently looked at that list, every single prayer request and dream has been fulfilled, except one. It was as if God went down the list and said, "Check, check, check..." Imagine that! What power! What love! Mind you, some of those requests and visions are seven years old. Biblically, that number means completion. Isn't our God amazing? Unbeknownst to me, those prayers were likely answered years ago in heaven but took seven years for the timing to be right on this earth!

He hasn't stopped surprising me. I don't share any of this to brag. The Lord knows I have nothing to boast about but Him. My heart is that these stories of God coming through and not only showing up but showing out will encourage you that He can and will do the same for you! We all need these reminders that God is real in daily life. The answers to your prayers may arrive in a different manner or process, but when God says, *"Now is the time,"* nothing can stop it. I believe it brings Him great joy and delight to run down that list of ours and allow them to come to fruition in the most spectacular and personal ways. Whether you are in the waiting or seeing Him answer your long-contended requests one by one before your very eyes, have faith to believe He will do it and won't stop until the answers reflect the beauty and perfection of heaven. I have no doubt He has a few surprises of His own to add to your prayers too! He is a benevolent God!

The Miracle of Restored Relationships

I have seen God restore friendships and relationships even within my family. There is unity, a new level of communication, and our faith has been strengthened and grown. My prayer for my family has been Psalm

1:1–3, and before my very eyes, I can see God bringing that to pass. I pray that verse over my future family too! The Lord opened the door to pray with a family member who also struggled with the spirit of fear. Had I not walked through that period of intense fear and warfare, I would not have been able to pray with them or relate. If God had done nothing else through this fairytale of a different variety, I testify that alone made the experience of battling fear and anxiety worth it!

The Miracle in my Health and Healing in my Soul

During writing this book, I started having symptoms in my abdominal area that were quite intense and uncommon for me. The issue was so bad that I had to see the doctor. (By now, you all know it had to be pretty bad for me to succumb to that!) As I sat on the floor of my bedroom one morning, laying hands on my abdomen while praying and declaring healing, I felt God say, *"This isn't the main thing. I need you to keep going."* I had peace and confidence that despite what I was feeling, this was not a big deal. The doctor recommended an ultrasound due to the quick onset of symptoms. I showed up to the ultrasound appointment like I was going to the hair salon. No fear. No anxiety. No worry. As I drove out of the hospital on this gloomy day, I had praise and worship music blaring when I looked up into the sky to see the sun breaking through an enormous dark cloud.

Again, I felt God whisper reassurance, *"I see where you are. I'm still here, and it is okay."* I smiled and sang a whole lot louder.

Several days passed and I hadn't anticipated hearing the results until the following week, but God brought the answer in record time. I was sitting at my kitchen island when the voicemail popped up—"Your results were normal." Those words washed over me, and I sobbed with relief and joy. Out loud, I said, "You were right, God! You were right!" Whatever the enemy was trying to bring against me, God made sure I knew it wasn't going to even be a thing! In this new era of the Spirit sweeping across the landscape of the world for revival and souls, miracles breaking out, and God taking us into new and wondrous things, I am confident the enemy will try to devour and hinder us in any way he can. May we tune our ears to heaven and listen to God's still small voice so that we hear the truth and advance by that and not be sidelined by the enemy! Had I not listened to God, the makings of this book would have been put back on the shelf to collect dust. I can guarantee it wouldn't have been written later either, but that is a *"Have You Ever?"* for another time!

On top of that experience, God brought it to my attention that I was free and healed. Every ounce of this fairytale at one time had haunted me. The people, warfare, circumstances, hurt, loss, and even some of the dreams and prophecies had become this secret that was holding me captive. I thought no one would understand and that I was the weird girl. I had concluded that I might be muzzled for the rest of my life about the events in Texas.

One morning in my prayer closet, after spending the previous day working on this book, I felt something, like a chunk of glass, break off me. I could literally feel it fall off. Hello, more freedom! If you have ever experienced that, you know it is the most incredible and indescribable feeling! He has made my heart whole and set me free. None of this has any power over me. Fear is gone. Anxiety no longer hinders me. Even my hair has been restored! It grows faster than I can keep up with and is healthier than ever. He has made that a crown upon my head, glistening with His glory, reminding the enemy every day that I was victorious! Can you imagine how infuriating that must be for him? I love it! What struck me to the core was that God made a point to tell me that I would share these stories with laughter and joy, and I can do that. This book is evidence of that very promise, and that could only happen because of Him.

The Miracle of Revival

Often God asks us to pray for things that may be totally out of our realm of earthly influence and are bigger than the happenings of daily life. Part of my prayer assignment was to intercede for repentance, revival, a fresh anointing, and the love of God to be evident and fall. I had no idea if God would allow me to witness or experience it, but one Sunday morning, I heard, "Go back." I did, but nothing stuck out to me except that everything was as it should be, and that gave me deep peace. Later, God gave me permission to return again, and low and behold, I witnessed it! The Holy Spirit was falling, moving in a fresh way, and touching the lives of those in His midst. You could see freedom breaking out (Where the Spirit of the Lord is, there is freedom (2 Corinthians 3:17, NIV)) and the love of God flowing from the hearts of those involved! The sanctuary was filled with new life, love, deeper faith, and purity! I felt the power of God wash over me as I worshiped, and it brought me to tears. He had done it! Prayers were answered! Revival was breaking out. This "shining city on a hill" had its light restored, and my heart couldn't have been happier. Every time I'm there, I am overcome with tears of gratefulness and sacred remembrance. It is a gift and makes every prayer-filled step in that old parking lot worth it.

The Miracle of the Ring

The final miracle is upon us, and it's a fitting end to this fairytale. One afternoon, on the way to the grocery store, I was at a familiar stoplight and had my left hand resting gently upon the top of my steering wheel.

I looked right and then slowly moved my eyes back to the left. At that moment, I was suddenly gazing upon a ring on my left-hand finger. I cannot tell you the specifics of the ring, only that it was present. I called a friend because, to be honest, I needed to confirm which hand an engagement ring would go on! Weddings and all that jazz have never enraptured me, and I am that girl who, although dreams of being married, the details are lost on me. God knows that I am oblivious, too.

After getting caught up in the details of being "Mrs. So and So," then having that not happen, I had asked God for purity in that department and for Him to help me forget anything that I had learned through that past relationship regarding weddings and diamonds. I wanted to be clean so that the events surrounding a future engagement and marriage would not be tainted. When God chose the person for me, the fun of that season would be a surprise. My prayer was for God to bring my husband and our marriage about miraculously to shout His glory and be holy ground, not manufactured with the "have to's" of this world.

It has been three years since the ring was placed upon my finger in that vision. Do I fully understand its significance? I highly doubt it, but that vision and ring are a gift from God confirming all that has been sealed in the Throne Room of heaven.

My promise-land is now my conquered land. (See, I told you the adventure was worth it! With God, it always will be.) This wild, promise-filled terrain was unexpected but more than I could have dreamed. God called San Antonio, Texas, my home, and although the promises within were important, it was also about my heart being home. I came for Jesus, but ultimately, He brought me for love. Now, I stand in a spacious place, having come full circle, with new dreams bubbling in my heart!

He has a promise-land for you too! He is leading you there with love, and you will conquer it! There is a specific inheritance for you in your promise-land (Joshua 23 and 24). You will stand in that land, whether physically or spiritually, and look back into His loving face with awe and exclaim, "I can't believe it! You did all this for me? I love it! Are you sure? How? Yes, Lord!" Your wonder will erupt, laughter will bubble over, and you will be elated by His plans for you. Where He leads will be captivating, and you'll experience God in the most profound and heartfelt ways. You won't ever want to let Him go, and you will treasure all He did for a lifetime. It will be that beautiful and full (with what I like to call the cream of the crop)! Don't be afraid to let Him hold the pen and craft your fairytale. Albeit one of a different variety—heavenly orchestrated, fit for a Queen, and nothing a traditional fairytale could ever hold a candle to.

This fairytale may be ending for now but scan the horizon for the next chapter because as the landscape changes, I hear the Lord heralding a new call, *"Do you want to come up a little higher?"* Sanctified. Set Apart. Healed. Free. Daughter of the King, your royal carriage awaits...

Verses to Declare:

> I have promised to rescue you from your oppression in Egypt. I will lead you to a land flowing with milk and honey.
>
> Exodus 3:17 (NLT)

> For you have given him his (insert your name) heart's desire; you have withheld nothing he (I) requested.
>
> Psalm 21:2 (NLT)

> Then Jesus said, "Did I not tell you that if you believe, you will see the glory of God?'"
>
> John 11:40 (NIV)

> Now then, stand still and see this great thing the Lord is about to do before your eyes!
>
> 1 Samuel 12:16 (NIV)

O Lord, I will honor and praise your name,
for you are my God. You do such wonderful
things! You planned them long ago, and now
you have accomplished them.

Isaiah 25:1 (NLT)

May God give you every desire of your heart
and carry out your every plan as you go to
battle. When you succeed, we will celebrate
and shout for joy. Flags will fly when victory is
yours! Yes, God will answer your prayers and
we will praise him! I know God gives me all
that I ask for and brings victory to his anointed king. My deliverance cry will be heard in
his holy heaven. By his mighty hand miracles
will manifest through his saving strength.

Psalm 20:4–6 (TPT)

Yes indeed, it won't be long now." God's Decree. "Things are going to happen so fast your
head will swim, one thing fast on the heels of
the other. You won't be able to keep up. Everything will be happening at once—and everywhere you look, blessings! Blessings like wine
pouring off the mountains and hills.

Amos 9:13–15 (MSG)

But Mary treasured up all these things and pondered them in her heart.

Luke 2:19 (NIV)

And now these three remain: faith, hope and love. But the greatest of these is love.

1 Corinthians 13:13 (NIV)

Prayer:

Lord Jesus, oh, Your love is so sweet. Your leading is wonderful beyond measure. I worship You today with my whole heart and, with a shout of jubilee, exclaim, "I have conquered the land!" You have placed a crown upon my head and fit me for the next chapter of my heavenly fairytale that will continue to boast of Your love and glory to the ends of the earth! Yes, Lord! Continue to write that story in my life! You promised I would see Your glory, and I have. You have done miracles! Thank you, Lord, for every great thing I have seen before my very eyes! Thank you for every battle! Each one equipped me for greater service and increased my capability to steward my new position and live out destiny. I stand in awe of You, forever grateful and filled with joy! You have changed my heart, given me new desires, and brought me full circle! Thank you, Jesus, for the changes I didn't even know I needed. They are all so precious to me. May I always honor and cherish You and what You have done. You are good, and You have been so good to me!

Take my hand, Lord, and lead me on to fully embrace the woman of God that You have made me be and the promises You have laid before me. Forever Your Daughter. Now a princess warrior turned queen—anointed and appointed. Take me higher, Lord! I declare I haven't seen anything yet! To God be the glory and all honor and fame be Yours forever. Amen!

THE END

Wait, you didn't think that was the end, did you? You haven't seen anything yet. Here's to a heavenly happily ever after!

Revelation 21:5 (NLT)
"And the one sitting on the throne said, "Look,
I am making everything new!" And then he said
to me, "Write this down, for what I tell you is
trustworthy and true."

Your Story— Activate and Accelerate

Some of you may have read this adventure and thought, "God doesn't speak to me. I don't have a God story. I don't have any spiritual gifts." I promise you that those statements couldn't be further from the truth. Before He fashioned you in your mother's womb, He knew you. He knew how your fairytale would play out on this earth and the talents and spiritual gifts He would bestow upon you. He also knows how to bring them to fruition and activate you to walk in them. He has given you a destiny and purpose for each gift.

When we accept Jesus Christ as our personal Lord and Savior, the Holy Spirit takes up residence in us (Ephesians 1:13, John 14:16–17, NLT). He comforts, guides, sanctifies, teaches, reminds us of truth, intercedes on our behalf, seals us as a believer in Jesus, enables us to live righteously and produce good fruit, provides understanding, revelation, and power. There are also the gifts of the Holy Spirit (1 Corinthians 12:1–11, NLT).

For me, God had to do a lot of teaching and maturing in my life before He could bring the gifts of the Holy Spirit to the forefront. It doesn't mean they weren't there or that I wasn't saved, but it wasn't time for me to focus on or operate in them fully. Like the Ecclesiastes verse noting times and seasons, that can be true of our spiritual gifts as well. Don't be discouraged if you feel like you can't see any of the gifts of the Spirit in your own life. You aren't behind. You aren't less than. God will bring them forth. He chooses the time and gifts, but we can always pray with sincere hearts to desire them all. How the Holy Spirit moves through us depends on our yielded heart and what is needed at the time. Sure, there are some spiritual gifts that we walk in regularly as part of our calling, but we are vessels, and when God wants something done on this earth, He only needs a willing heart. If we remain connected to God and pursue purity (remove sin), then the Holy Spirit can flow freely through us. God's will is that we walk in those spiritual gifts and the authority, anointing, and calling He has placed on our lives. But first and foremost, He wants to be our first love. Jesus first. Everything else is second! (Don't get that backward. It won't go well!)

Your story will be different than mine, and that is precisely how it should be! You are unique, and He will speak and train you in ways that you will understand, with, of course, the foundation being the Bible. He won't ever go against His Word when leading, teaching, or training. He is the best teacher you will ever have.

Today, I encourage you to kneel and humbly ask God to reveal how He would like to express Himself to and through you for such a time as this! It is the heart of the Father to make Himself known and build His Church! Seek His face. He will meet with you. He wants to! As you seek Him, know that He will answer about your spiritual gifts and destiny too. He is already proud of you, regardless of where you are in your journey, but He also wants to do so much more! We get the privilege of partnering with Him, but He gets all the glory!

Verses to Declare:

Now, dear brothers and sisters, regarding your question about the special abilities the Spirit gives us. I don't want you to misunderstand this. You know that when you were still pagans, you were led astray and swept along in worshiping speechless idols. So I want you to know that no one speaking by the Spirit of God will curse Jesus, and no one can say Jesus is Lord, except by the Holy Spirit. There are different kinds of spiritual gifts, but the same Spirit is the source of them all. There are different kinds of service, but we serve the same Lord. God works in different ways, but it is the same God who does the work in all of us. A spiritual gift is given to each of us so we can help each other. To one person the Spirit gives the ability to give wise advice; to another the same Spirit gives a message of special knowledge. The same Spirit gives great faith to another, and to someone else the one Spirit gives the gift of healing. He gives one person the power to perform miracles, and another the ability to prophesy. He gives someone else the ability to discern whether a message is from the Spirit of God or from another spirit. Still another person is given the ability to speak in unknown languages, while another is given the ability to interpret what is being said. It is the one and only Spirit who distributes all these gifts. He alone decides which gift each person should have.

1 Corinthians 12:1–11 (NLT)

My sheep hear my voice, and I know them, and they follow me. I give them eternal life, and they will never perish, and no one will snatch them out of my hand. My Father, who has given them to me, is greater than all, and no one is able to snatch them out of the Father's hand. I and the Father are one.

John 10:27–30 (ESV)

Jesus answered, "I am the way, and the truth, and the life. No one comes to the Father except through me."

John 14:6 (NIV)

When the Spirit of truth comes, he will guide you into all truth, for he will not speak on his own authority, but whatever he hears he will speak, and he will declare to you the things that are to come. He will glorify me, for he will take what is mine and declare it to you.

John 16:13–14 (ESV)

Let love be your highest goal! But you should also desire the special abilities the Spirit gives—especially the ability to prophesy.

1 Corinthians 14:1 (NLT)

Prayer:

Heavenly Father, sometimes it can be tough to come home to You because of my pride, guilt, shame, and misconceptions, but because of Your Son, Jesus Christ, You welcome me with open arms. If I haven't made the decision to follow You, I would like to do that. I confess that I am a sinner and need You as my Savior. I believe that You sent Your one and only Son, Jesus Christ, to die for me so that I may have eternal life. I believe He rose from the dead and sits at the right hand of the Father. I repent of my sins— even the ones that are hard to turn away from - and ask for forgiveness. Help me to forsake those things that grieve You, God. Today, I give You my life and heart and receive Jesus as my Savior. I declare He is my Lord— the way, the truth, and the life! Thank you, God, for Your Son and His precious blood that was shed to save me! I am now a Daughter of the Most High God and belong to Your kingdom! (All of heaven is rejoicing!)

As a believer, Lord, I want to walk in intimacy with You all the days of my life. Thank you for giving me the Holy Spirit and the promise that He lives in me! Lord Jesus, please continually fill me with Your love and power! I want to know Your voice and hear You, and I desire all the gifts of the Spirit, including prophecy. Please bring these gifts to life in me so I can walk in the fullness of them and everything that You paid for on the Cross. Not for my gain or fame but for Your glory alone.

Lastly, please ignite in me the courage to share my story of what You have done in my life! May shame, guilt, embarrassment, fear, and spiritual warfare never keep me from releasing what You have put inside of me. Please give me the words You want me to share. Activate and accelerate me, Lord, into every plan and purpose for my life. Your kingdom come, and Your will be done on earth as it is in heaven. In Your great and wonderful name, Jesus, amen!

Your "Have You Ever?"

Have you ever...had a God story? I have no doubt you do! I wish I could hear yours! Maybe you are ready to share it too! The Bible says, "There is a season for everything and a time for every activity under heaven" (Ecclesiastes 3:1, NLT, paraphrased). For whatever reason, this is the season for my story to be penned. I believe now may be the time to share yours too!

In this process, I have noticed one theme prevalent in believers' lives when I ask them about their story—many are reluctant to share. Some don't know what to say. For others, there is shame, fear, self-protection, embarrassment, self-consciousness, and as a result, they haven't experienced their full freedom and the multiplication of joy and healing meant to go forth from their stories. They have been muzzled, and their stories are bound tightly and hidden away in the depths of their souls. Honestly, it has stirred a new fire inside of me because I was one of those people. I never knew how much I was being rendered ineffective or how much the enemy had used the circumstances of my life to keep me silent.

Yes, there is a God-ordained time. Yes, there may even be aspects of your life's journey that God never asks you to share, and that is alright. There is also a way to share and honor God and the people who have graced your life. Be wise and have discernment. We always want to be kind, gracious, loving, classy, and respectful. But completely silent, cowering and shrinking back when God says to speak. No. Not today. Not anymore.

The Bible says, "We overcome him (the Devil) by the blood of the Lamb and by the word of our testimony" (Revelation 12:11, NKJV). We are all sinners and need the blood of the Lamb (Jesus) to remove our sins and defeat the Devil's hold on us. Only Jesus could do that for us. Then comes your testimony! Only you can share that.

This book is a testimony of God's grace, faithfulness, love, the miraculous, and more. I am an overcomer, and so are you! Every time we share what God has done, we conquer the enemy, break the chains of bondage, our faith increases, and God gets more glory! Do you know what else it does? Every time you share what He has done in your life, the world finds hope and the answers they have been looking for all along—our good God! Our testimonies point people to the Gospel and reveal His nature. They bring God to life in real-time! This intensely parched, love- and truth-starved world needs that more than ever before! What a blessing God has given us to be able to share what He has done!

The verse God gave that confirmed I was supposed to embrace writing this fairytale of a different variety was Psalm 96:3 (NLT): "Publish his glorious deeds among the nations. Tell everyone about the amazing things he does." I encourage you to do the same with your story. You are being called to the frontlines to speak, testify, minister the Gospel, and lead people to Jesus! Your story has a significant part in the narrative unfolding in this world. A harvest and souls are attached to it! The enemy is terrified by what God wants to do through it, but God wants you to take your place! I declare over you today if you were like me and felt muzzled, that the war on your voice has ended, and you are being let loose in Jesus' name to share what God has done!

You Are Invited...

To share your fairytale of a different variety! If you have a God story to share, please visit "Have You Ever?" on Facebook via this link https://www.facebook.com/haveyouever2020/. Long before this book was going to be published, God dropped these words into my spirit, *"Gather My kids to share what I have done in their lives,"* and we have done just that! We would love to hear yours, too, and celebrate what God has done in your life. Hope to see you there!

Bibliography

Alles, Roger, Minkoff, Rob, dir. *The Lion King*. 1996; Burbank, CA: Walt Disney Pictures, 1994. DVD.

Bethel Music, "Goodness of God" 2018, track #2 on *Victory*, Bethel Music, 2019. CD.

Breathitt, Barbie L, Dr. *A to Z Dream Symbology Dictionary*. For Numbers Referenced in Text. Altona: Friesens, 2015.

Couch, Andrae, "Take Me Back," 1973, track #523 on *The New Church Hymnal*, Lexicon Music Group, Inc, 1976, Hymnal.

Daigle, Lauren and The Belonging, Co, "Peace Be Still (Live)" 2019, track #4 on *All the Earth*, TBCO Music, 2019. CD.

Geronimi, Clyde, Jackson, Wildfred, Luske, Hamilton, dir. *Cinderella*. 1950; Burbank, CA: Walt Disney Productions, 1950. Film.

Knecht, Alicia. *Sparky and Millie's Ocean Adventure*. Mustang: Tate Publishing, 2015.

Lewis, C. S. "The Four Loves (Storge or Affection)," CS Lewis Doodle YouTube Video. 27.30. May 14, 2017.

Lewis, C. S. "The Four Loves (Philia or Friendship)," CS Lewis Doodle YouTube Video. 30:29. August 11, 2017.

Lewis, C. S. "The Four Loves (Eros or The Love Between the Sexes)," CS Lewis Doodle YouTube Video. 36:37. November 11, 2017.

Lewis, C. S. "The Four Loves (Agape or God's Love)," CS Lewis Doodle YouTube Video. 27:47. May 5, 2018.

Martin, CD, Gabriel, Charles, "His Eye Is on the Sparrow," 1905, Hymnal.

McLean, Don, "American Pie," 1971, track #1 on *American Pie*, United Artists Records, 1971. Vinyl.

Moore, Beth. *The Quest: An Excursion Toward Intimacy with God*. Nashville: Lifeway Press, 2017.

Moore, Beth. *When Ungodly People Do Ungodly Things: Arming Yourself in the Age of Seduction*. Nashville: Lifeway Press, 2005.

Shirer, Priscilla. *Jonah: Navigating a Life Interrupted*. Nashville: Lifeway Press, 2010.

Shirer, Priscilla. *The Armor of God.* Nashville: Lifeway Press, 2015.

Strong, James LLD, STD. "Yadah." *The New Strongs Expanded Exhaustive Concordance of the Bible.* Nashville: Thomas Nelson. 2001.

Waller, John, "Something Big," 2007, track #9 on *The Blessing*, Reunion Records, 2007, CD.

Wilkinson, Bruce. *The Dream Giver: Following Your God-Given Destiny.* New York City: Multnomah, 2003.

About the Author

Alicia Knecht is a big fan of life and laughter. She has a passion for people to know Jesus, be healed, set free, see His miracles in everyday life, and for their destiny to come to pass. She is the Founder of A Strong and Healthy Life and the Have You Ever? testimonial ministry. She published a children's book called *Sparky and Millie's Ocean Adventure* and hopes to continue writing, sharing God stories, and encouraging others in the future.

CPSIA information can be obtained
at www.ICGtesting.com
Printed in the USA
BVHW070215250522
637945BV00013B/384